RAMBLINGS
OF
A 21ST CENTURY HUMAN
(VOLUME ONE)

I.M. HUMAN

Ramblings of a 21st Century Human

Volume 1

Ramblings of a 21st Century Human

Volume 1

I.M. Human

Contents

About the Author

As one might expect the author is, indeed, human. The author writes in the 3rd person when penning a section like this one, giving the impression that someone else wrote it, as that is what humans typically do in these situations. Born on Earth more than 10,000 but less than 20,000 days ago, Human likes to be vague when it comes to his identity. Human, entrepreneur and writer are some of the nouns most commonly used to describe I.M., however, some less used but probably more accurate descriptions would be perpetual thinker and constant student.

Dedication

Dedicated to my best human friend, who also happens to be my spouse, (much) better half and significant other.

Q. What is black & white, read all over, and costs less than 12 Chicken Nuggets?

A. The digital version of this book. (100% Guaranteed to teach you more than a dozen bite-size pieces of dead poultry!)

Preface

I have been disappointed, as of late, with many of the digital works being released on the market today, claiming to be books but merely a few pages long, containing minimal content and churned out at a very rapid rate, as if to beat the system and essentially fooling their readers in the process. There are even websites selling ways to "write" 7 books in 7 days, and tips on how to trick people into buying them. When I first decided to write this series there was only one rule – never compromise the reading experience by taking shortcuts. Each book has a lot of hours, days, weeks and months behind it and the formula will never change.

Ramblings are said to be meandering talks that go from one subject to another without any clear purpose or direction. This might indeed be true in the case of this series, however even though the subjects might not be related to one another, the purpose of them is one; to give something back to the reader that can be shared with other humans. There are countless undisputed truths here, but also a few open questions.

This is a different kind of book. Everybody has that one friend that you end up learning a thing or two from every time you meet, and if you don't have one, you really should! Each book in the series is full of thoughts, facts, opinions, puzzles, ideas, quotes, riddles, jokes, games, tips, tricks, recipes and anything else that can be absorbed or conjured up by the mind *of a 21st century human.* At the end of each book there is also a quiz which can be attempted alone, but would be even better organized as a competition with other humans who have read the book as well as those who have not.

If you like this book, please do tell other humans about it just by leaving a review. It takes no time at all and would be invaluable to me and help me to continue the series. It will also help me to improve future content by being able to invest more time in the project, conduct more research and allow me to include copyrighted images for example, that would need to be paid for.

Thank you.

I.M Human

Chapter 1: It's A Boy. Buy Him A Pink Dress!

As humans, we sometimes take certain things for granted in life. We assume that things are just the way they are because that's how they always were and that is how they always will be. Well at least I did! The truth is that every little detail about this life we lead has a history, and throughout this series I will be addressing many topics that revolve around this theme, that is, common facts which we may take for granted that have very interesting and less celebrated backstories. If someone had to shout out the following words and ask you to quickly associate colours with them, how would you reply?

BOY   **GIRL**   **STOP**   **GO**

Let us look at the first two words, boy and girl. The most common colours associated with them nowadays are the gender-specific blue and pink, we will get to the words stop and go later. It all started with the clothing industry. Before inexpensive dyes that allowed clothes to be washed multiple times without fading were invented, most children simply wore white clothes, white dresses to be specific, regardless of whether the child was male or female. They were seen as practical in terms of cleaning as they would just bleach the white dress if dirty. Dresses also allowed for more flexibility when changing the child and did not need to fit perfectly, so would last longer. It was normal for children of both sexes to wear white dresses until the age of 6 years.

When these cheap dyes came into existence, clothes started being produced primarily in pastel colours, but there were no strict guidelines on what colours children would wear, let alone whether boys and girls should have different coloured clothes. These had to be made up as society evolved. One of the earliest gender-specific colour suggestions can be found in the June 1918 edition of the trade publication Earnshaw's Infants' Department: "There has been a great diversity of opinion on the subject, but the generally accepted rule is pink for the boy and blue for the girl. The reason is that pink being a more decided and stronger colour is more suitable for the boy, while blue, which is more delicate and dainty, is prettier for the girl."

Dressmaker magazine printed something similar: "The preferred colour to dress young boys in is pink. Blue is reserved for girls as it is considered paler and the more dainty of the two colours, and pink is thought to be stronger (akin to red)." This general understanding persisted until the late 1920s.

Time Magazine in 1927 described how Princess Astrid of Belgium had been caught off-guard when she gave birth to a baby girl, as "the cradle had been optimistically outfitted in pink, the colour for boys." That same year Time Magazine published a colour chart based on the suggestions of some of the biggest retailers in the US. All retailers said pink was the colour for boys and blue the colour for girls. This so called advice was presumably nothing but a sly marketing technique though, so that parents with both boys and girls would now need to spend more money and buy different coloured clothing, rather than being able to wear their older sibling's hand-me-downs. Sneaky humans!

These particular gender-specific colour associations lasted until World War II. The exact reason for this is not confirmed but the main consensus is that Adolf Hitler was responsible for this change. When the Nazis separated homosexual men from straight men in the concentration camps, they put pink triangles on the clothing of those homosexuals that apparently could be "cured" from their ways. As a result, the colour pink became more feminine and by the end of World War II the colour recommendations were reversed, it was now blue for boys and pink for girls.

This trend lasted until the 1960s, when feminists decided that females should wear whatever colour they liked and there should not be any specific colours. In fact, fashion became rather unisex, with women opting for non-feminine and more neutral attires and clothing companies adapted to these changes by the 1970s. This was all to change again in the 1980s though, when gender-specific colours were re-introduced by retailers once again looking to make more money. Greedy humans! This time around, the colours went far beyond clothing. Pre-natal testing that allowed parents to find out the gender of their baby, allowed parents to buy gender-specific coloured products before the baby was even born. Prams, cots, toys and baby furniture could now be gender-specific and would not be able to be reused if parents had children of different sexes. The trend is still present nowadays as can be very clearly seen if you walk into any clothing or toy store, and does not seem to be losing any steam, at least for the time being.

Could one man, Adolf Hitler, really be the cause of a switch in society's views of two colours though? Yes! In fact he has changed people's perception of many things that still stand today, so I do not find it so far-fetched. Did you know that the swastika symbol was a sacred symbol way before it was a symbol that represented pure evil? Earliest traces of the symbol itself date back to 10,000 BC and can still be seen as an important symbol in Hinduism and Buddhism to date. The word itself is derived from the Sanskrit words "su" meaning 'well' and "asti" meaning 'being', to form 'well-being'. How can a symbol representing good fortune for thousands of years be easily changed by one man into a symbol of hate, and should it remain that way? Are we letting evil triumph over good by only acknowledging the bad connotations rather than the positive ones?

A fashion designer by the name of Sinjun Wessin recently tried to re-introduce the original good meaning of the swastika into Western culture. "If the hate is taken away from the symbol by energizing its positive side, then we take away power from the people who want to use it in a hateful way", Wessin said. I completely agree with this sentiment to be honest. One human should not have the power to dictate whether or not something should be seen as good or evil. Some thinkers, however, believe that it is the right only of those affected by the Nazis to decide what to do with it, and most of these victims are not on the same wavelength as Wessin. They believe that the symbol is so tainted that it will never be able to take on its original meaning ever again. Thank you Hitler for ruining the swastika symbol for everyone, just like you ruined the tooth-brush moustache that was so loved when Charlie Chaplin and Oliver Hardy wore it!

You probably would answer red and green, when asked for the most common colours associated with stop and go. This is due to the various signage seen nowadays, something that most people see on a daily basis, especially on traffic lights.

The blue light marks the crippled car,

The green light signals slow;

The red light is a danger light,

The white light, "Let her go."

The above extract is from a 1911 poem by Cy Warman called "Will the Lights be White?" It is evident when reading it that red and green did not always represent stop and go. As far back as the 1830s, different railway yards used many different systems of signalling. In 1841, engineer Henry Booth devised a colour scheme that would be standard all around Britain, proposing red for "stop", white for "go" and green for "caution". The selection of white as being the colour for "go" ended up causing problems. In 1914 for example, a red lens fell off the signal box leaving only a white light. This caused the train to run a stop signal and crash into another train with devastating consequences. From then on, white was removed, green was switched with it to represent "go" and yellow was introduced instead to represent "caution", probably because of the contrast between all colours.

The modern day traffic lights colour scheme was imported from the railroad system and Britain was the first country to use traffic lights on roads. In 1868 the first crude version of traffic lights were installed and these had to be operated by a policeman. These lights, red and green, were powered by gas running though pipes and were not without their own problems, with one of the lights exploding and injuring a policeman after just one month. It was not until 1920, across the Atlantic in the US, in Detroit, that policeman William Potts invented the first 3 colour traffic light, using the same colours and meanings used in the railway industry, red, green and yellow. We can only wonder the main reasons why red and green were initially chosen, apart from being strong colours that stand out and contrast with each other, we can definitely find that throughout history, colour representation always associated red with danger, probably because of the connotations with blood and fire. Green probably was chosen for more scientific and practical reasons rather than symbolic ones. Let us just hope that the traffic light colours we have today are here to stay, as this will undoubtedly cause mass confusion, similar to what happened on September 3rd 1967, when Sweden decided to start driving on the right side of the road instead of the left, resulting in chaos!

Chapter 2: Mile High

Today I woke up 36,000 feet in the air (that's around 11,000 meters). A very 21st century thing to say indeed. As I darted through the sky in this highly flammable metal tube I wondered if this was really the best humans could do? I mean it is a great feat, no doubt about that, but maybe one day we will look back fondly and remember the days of travel by airplane, which by then would have been replaced by much more advanced and safer modes of transport. Teleportation perhaps? My father used to tell me wonderful stories about teleportation as a child, saying that by the time I would become an adult it would be commonplace, but alas we have yet to see such a thing. I am beginning to wonder if I ever will ever see this in my lifetime. He also told me stories about wristwatches that would enable you to communicate instantly with other humans, which, as you probably know have now been invented, so at least my childhood bedtime stories had a little truth in them after all.

In all fairness, upon giving air travel nowadays a closer inspection, it really isn't that bad at all. Even though people fear it more than any other mode of transport that exists (probably due to the flammable metal tube in the sky part), the statistics don't lie. Air travel is the safest form of transport out there. To understand why this is so, one must first comprehend the scale of commercial air travel in the 21st century. At any single point in time there are more than 6000 commercial passenger airplanes flying about Earth, a great way to visualize this is by using Flightradar24's website (www.flightradar24.com) or app. Flights per year? More than 30 million. Let those figures sink in for a while. Accidents are very, very rare. 2013 was the safest year for air travel since the 1940s, with

265 deaths recorded worldwide. You can do the math of the probability of you dying in an airplane crash... or I could just tell you, the odds are around 1 in 10 million. The odds of you dying in a car accident in any given year is about 1 in 10,000. Unfortunately the cliché is true, you are more likely to get killed driving to the airport than on an airplane!

That being said, airplane fatalities are not usually your fault, whereas a majority of car crash fatalities can be directly attributed to a driver, which many a time could be you. Of course there are ways to reduce these odds, for example you should not use your mobile phone while driving, never drive when tired, always wear a seat belt and never ever drive under the influence. As a passenger on an airplane on the other hand, you do not have any say in swaying the odds of potential disaster in your favour, so this is probably why so many people are scared of air travel. The feeling of not being in control. They would rather get behind the wheel of a car, with 100 times a greater risk of dying, as long as they are in control... or at least think they are!

Another promising statistic to keep in mind is that even in the rare instance that your airplane is involved in a crash, you have a 90% chance of surviving, which is quite amazing. Enough morbid talk for now though, as I think we can all agree that the fear of flying (aviophobia or aerophobia), which affects up to 1 In 5 people, can correctly be considered a relatively irrational fear to have in the 21st century. The truth is though, even the most hardened air traveller can sometimes get a bit uncomfortable, especially when the aircraft encounters such things as turbulence. What is turbulence though and can it be so bad that it causes damage?

There are number of different types of turbulence that exist. You might need to bear with me for just a little bit here because I believe it is important to understand certain things properly. The most common type of turbulence encountered is Clear Air Turbulence (CAT). In the sky there are long stretches of horizontal air known as jet streams, sort of like roads on land. Now these jet streams can either be flowing in the plane's direction (headwind), so they should be avoided, or else going in the same direction as the plane (tailwind). The plane would enter this jet stream if it is a tailwind, to be given a push so to speak, and in turn save fuel. The sides of the jet stream can sometimes mix with other air which would be moving at a different speed and this would produce turbulence. Wake turbulence is another type of turbulence which is man-made however, rather than natural, and it can occur when another aircraft flying in front of yours disturbs the air flow. Usually the bigger the plane the more wake turbulence it can cause and that is in fact why air traffic control imposes minimum distances to be kept from each other depending on plane size. This is very similar to what happens when small boats are rocked by bigger ones when they pass by them.

Pilots cannot really detect turbulence but can usually avoid it with the help of other pilots who just went through the same route and pass on this information to each other and to air traffic control. Routes can then be changed if it is going to be particularly uncomfortable, otherwise the flight will go ahead as planned. Pilots usually do not avoid turbulence because it is dangerous, they just want you, as a passenger, to be relaxed at all times and not spill your fruit juice! Turbulence has a scale from light, moderate to severe. Light and Moderate turbulence will feel a bit uncomfortable for a passenger but is not at all dangerous. Severe turbulence is very rare, but nowadays isn't really dangerous as airplanes are built much sturdier than they used to be. It might be dangerous to you as a passenger if your seatbelt is not on though and this is in fact why airlines recommend you keep your seatbelt at all times, even when the remove seatbelt sign has come on. The cabin crew are not just trying to annoy you! The likelihood of encountering severe turbulence is around 1 in a million though. Another comforting statistic.

Still, even in the worst turbulence don't expect the airplanes wings to snap off, as planes go through extreme tests before allowing passengers to get into them. Some tests include applying 150% greater force on the wings than the plane would normally encounter and the wing would actually bend up to 24 feet (7 meters) and still remain intact! Another test that humans conduct is shooting dead chickens at the plane's engines and windshield to simulate birds colliding with a plane, which is known as a bird strike. The chicken gun (great name) as it is called, is basically a large diameter compressed-air cannon that shoots chickens at an aircraft to make sure it still functions normally in case the aircraft encounters a flock of geese for example. Legend has it that the British borrowed this technology from the US to test their windshields, but none of them were passing the test. Upon asking the US to see what could be wrong, one recommendation was sent back to Britain, "use a thawed chicken!"

The sensation of the plane descending rapidly that you feel shortly after take-off is another feeling that many passengers, me included, do not particular like, but thankfully it is just an illusion. The feeling is brought about by a change of speed in the climb or a levelling off of the aircraft rather than an actual descent. Immediately after take-off this is usually caused by speed restrictions, depending on the altitude, as well as noise reduction procedures that are required at some airports. There could also be cases where air traffic control would instruct the plane to stop climbing as there would be another plane above it, so the pilot would climb slower and then level off, creating the illusion of falling since your body would have got used to climbing at the faster speed. The feeling could be compared to being on an elevator headed to the 20th floor of a building. As it approaches the 20th floor it would start to slow down and your body would feel like the elevator is actually falling rather than going up. In fact, pilots are trained to trust their instruments over their natural instinct, as the human body can misinterpret feelings easily. If only humans had accurate instruments for measuring other things, such as love!

The sinking feeling that you usually get mid-flight, when the airplane dips suddenly is actually pilot correction to avoid turbulence. Many passengers use the term 'air-pocket' when describing this sensation but there technically is no such thing as an air pocket. Although many passengers think that they are falling from the sky very rapidly, the most you would ever move up or down in a commercial airplane is around 20 feet (6 meters). There seems to be this misconception that some areas in the sky are devoid of air, and that airplanes that pass through them fall for a while until they reach the next level of air. This is completely incorrect and areas without any air in them do not exist in the sky. Think of the sky like the sea, there are no water pockets in the sea that are devoid of water. A trick that you can use to avoid the sinking feeling is to tense your stomach muscles when you feel it. Otherwise you can just embrace it, people do pay for rollercoaster rides after all!

Another thing that always used to arouse my curiosity was the series of sounds, dings and dongs that would come on at any given time during the flight and what they meant. Was this a secret code from the cockpit telling the flight attendants to prepare for disaster? Not usually the case. These sounds are actually called chimes and they usually vary from airline to airline and they can mean a variety of things. They are how the cockpit communicates with the cabin crew, how the cabin crew call each other from opposite ends of the plane (like a telephone), the chime you make when you press the button over you to call a member of the cabin crew and also common safety alerts such as fasten seatbelts. Without going into too much detail, these sounds should not cause any undue stress, especially if they are single or dual chimes. In the *unlikely event* (to use a phrase airlines love using) that you ever had to hear a consecutive number of chimes, possibly 5 in quick succession, you may need to put your book down. Statistically though, the worst thing you should ever hear in a lifetime of flying on a commercial passenger airplane is that they have run out of your favourite red wine!

Chapter 3: Just A Spoon Full Of Sugar... Or 9

Imagine this, you wake up in the morning and start making your coffee or tea and proceed to put in a teaspoon of sugar, and another one, and another one... until you drop in 9 teaspoons of sugar. Sounds crazy right? But this is exactly how much sugar you are putting into your body when you drink one SMALL can of regular cola. A small can of cola has around 38g of sugar and one teaspoon of sugar is equal to 4g of the stuff. We should really distinguish between naturally occurring sugars and added sugars though, good and bad sugars.

Naturally occurring sugars can be found in milk (lactose) and in fruit and vegetables (fructose) for example. When you consume these products you are taking in sugar in its natural state along with a whole lot of other ingredients, vitamins and minerals. In milk for example, along with the lactose you are consuming such things as calcium and Vitamin D which aids with sugar metabolism. Fructose in fruit and vegetables should also be seen in the context of eating the fruit or vegetable as a whole, since they are high in fibre which also aids sugar metabolism. This means that when you drink freshly squeezed orange juice you are taking away most of the fibre and simply drinking the liquid which is also full of sugar, so technically it would be better to consume an orange whole, rather than in juice form.

Added sugars are definitely what we need to worry about. These are the sugars that are added to processed food and drinks, and they are all over the place. They have no nutritional value and are basically added to make anything taste, look and feel better than they really should. Added sugars are essentially empty calories, which means that they provide energy but no nutrition. The over consumption of these added sugars, which are extremely hard to avoid nowadays, is linked to the ever-increasing risk of cardiovascular disease, diabetes, high blood pressure and obesity. In 1822, Americans consumed around 45 grams of sugar every 5 days, compared to a whopping 765 grams every 5 days nowadays (according to a 2012 study). That's 17 times more than 1822. An average of 38 teaspoons of sugar a day. Are you still finding it hard to link excess sugar to medical problems?

To put things into perspective, it is recommended that men have 9 teaspoons of added sugar a day whereas women should have just 6 teaspoons! These added sugars can come in many forms and could even be naturally occurring like white sugar and honey, or manufactured ones such as high fructose corn syrup. The problem is that there are so many names for these added sugars that you won't even realize unless you take a really close look. Here are just a few of the names they go by:

Agave nectar, Brown sugar, Cane crystals, Cane sugar, Coconut sugar, Confectioner's sugar, Corn sweetener, Corn syrup, Crystalline fructose, Dextrose, Evaporated cane juice, Organic evaporated cane juice, Fructose, Fruit juice concentrates, Galactose, Glucose, Granulated Sugar, High-fructose corn syrup, Invert sugar, Lactose, Maltose, Malt sugar, Malt syrup, Maple Syrup, Molasses, Raw sugar, Sucrose, Sugar, Syrup, Turbinado sugar.

Devious humans! Added sugar everywhere, hidden in all types of processed foods. One single tablespoon of tomato ketchup has around one teaspoon of sugar in it! Even food labelling can be rather misleading. The label 'No added sugars' might make someone think that there is no sugar in the product for example, but they would still have natural sugars in it from milk or fruit. It is not easy to completely avoid sugars in our diet but we can at least try and moderate our intake. Every human's daily calorie intake is different depending on gender, age, height, weight and how physically active they are. If you search for 'calorie calculator' on the Internet you can easily calculate your recommended daily calorie intake. The rule of thumb for finding out how many calories in any given amount of grams of added sugar is by multiplying by 4 (1g of sugar = 4 calories). Therefore a small can of cola with 38g of sugar amounts to 152 calories. If you have a recommended calorie intake of 2000 calories you should not go over that amount per day even on nutritious foods but if you consume less, for example 1800 calories then you would have 200 discretionary calories to use on these empty calories. The more of an active life-style you lead the more calories you need per day and as a result the more discretionary calories you could technically afford. I would completely cut out these empty calories, even if I could afford it, but each to his own!

How does sugar make humans overweight though? One word. Insulin. To be fair, without insulin you would not survive as it is the hormone that the pancreas produces to get rid of the sugar in your blood. The trick here is to not force your body to constantly produce insulin, as this is where problems begin. If you are trying to lose weight and be healthy, forget all these fancily named diets and just remember these words: reduce the insulin in your body. Sugars are part of the carbohydrate family which also include starch and cellulose. When you eat sugar, or any other carbohydrate your body converts it into glucose which enters your blood stream and as a result your blood sugar level rises. When insulin comes into the equation your body starts burning sugar instead of your fat and the burned sugar is stored up as fat, so your body will never get a chance to burn off your actual fat. It might sound strange at first but it could be better to cut down on excess sugar and other carbohydrates rather than fat for example. Of course, moderation is always key. There is a great measure called the Glycemic Index (GI) which measures a particular food's effect on your blood sugar. The lower the GI, the less insulin produced.

I feel very strongly about reducing sugars because I believe it is something that the food industry is forcing upon us while covering up the negative effects it has on our bodies for their own gain. My father once told me that if humans had lungs on the outside of their bodies they would probably never smoke. Sugar is causing very noticeable effects to our bodies, humans are getting fat, very fat, yet we do not seem to care or maybe we simply do not believe that sugar is the cause. 92% of Americans aged 20-64 also have some form of tooth decay, which is undoubtedly sugar related. Humans did not always have bad teeth though. Scientists studying remains of the victims from the Mount Vesuvius eruption in Pompeii discovered that they had perfect teeth and this was way before toothpaste or toothbrushes were invented! They believe the reason for this was probably their very low sugar diet.

How can we reduce our sugar intake easily? Cut down slowly. Try replacing certain sugary foods with fruit and sugary drinks with water, you do not need to go cold turkey, just start reducing gradually. It does not help that sugar is nearly as addictive as cocaine but with enough willpower it can be done. If you can't do it alone try doing this with another human. Avoid giving sugars to children at a young age, cravings for sugars will build up over time so do not let that happen. Also, eating a sugary snack can be linked to simply being bored, so keep yourself busy and you will not even think of sugar. If you really really need something to sweeten your next tea or coffee it might be wise to consider an artificial sweetener such as saccharine, many experts recommend this as an alternative to sugar. Claims that artificial sweeteners are harmful are inconclusive and they are still considered as less damaging than sugar. The facts are there, too much sugar is bad for you, very bad for you. So do your body a favour, don't listen to Mary Poppins, and cut down on that sugar now before it's too late!

Chapter 4: As easy as ABC?

Used every day, these symbols have become a foundation of human existence without which our lives would not be able to function as seamlessly as they do. These instantly recognizable 26 shapes can be arranged in an infinite number of combinations to express limitless ideas and emotions. We are of course talking about the glyphs in the alphabet, more specifically, the English alphabet. You probably heard about the alphabet from that catchy song right? You know, the song you hear when you press 1 1 9 9 # # 9 6 6 3 3 2 2 2 2 1 9 9 6 3 3 2 999 6 3 3 2 1 1 9 9 # # 9 6 6 3 3 2 2 1 on a telephone keypad. Which come to think of it has the exact same tune as Twinkle Twinkle Little Star and Baa Baa Black Sheep... OK moving along. While reading this book you may have probably noticed some of these graphemes (the smallest unit of any language's writing system) scattered around in various orders...

Letters of the alphabet! I knew there was an easier word for them! How did these letters come to be and why did we settle on the 26 that form the English alphabet as we know it? To answer this we need to go way back to around 3000 BC when the Sumerians were using cuneiform and the Egyptians were using hieroglyphics to represent sounds used to communicate. This was the first record of symbols being physically produced to represent sounds, but it was not exactly an alphabet as we know it today because theses cuneiforms and hieroglyphics did not represent single units of sounds (or phonemes) but groups of sounds (words). So one symbol would have represented the word 'sun' for instance. As humans advanced, this form of writing was not seen as very practical anymore, because this system meant that you would have to memorize an enormous number of different symbols.

The Canaanite script, also known as the Proto-Sinaitic script developed around the years 1800-1900 BC, once again in Ancient Egypt and was heavily influenced by Egyptian hieratic. It was a cursive script (written with joined characters) that allowed the Egyptians to save time by not having to go through the longer process of using hieroglyphics. While the Canaanite alphabet was probably the first true alphabet in the sense that it consisted of single units of sounds, it had one major difference to the alphabet of today, that it only consisted of consonants and had no vowels whatsoever so the reader had to basically guess what vowel to use while reading. The game Wheel of Fortune would definitely be much harder with this system! This consonantal type of alphabet is often referred to as an abjad (a term suggested by scholar Peter T. Daniels), to distinguish it from alphabets that feature vowels, which are known as phonetic alphabets, or true alphabets if you will. The Phoenicians built upon this Canaanite alphabet and standardized an alphabet consisting of 22 letters, still lacking vowels. As the Phoenician civilization spread, so did their alphabet, and due to their maritime nature and the fact that they were master traders, it reached as far as the Mediterranean and Southern Europe, influencing some very important cultures, most importantly for this chapter, the Greeks.

It was the Greeks who took the alphabet that the Phoenicians were spreading around and improved upon it round about the year 1000 BC, inserted vowels into it (which turned out to be pretty useful) and ended up creating the first true alphabet. When the Greeks exported this great new alphabet to Italy it evolved into the Latin alphabet after the Romans had combined it with characters from the Etruscan alphabet. It continued to develop into an alphabet that pretty much resembles the present day English alphabet until around AD 500, when it contained nearly every letter except J, U, V and W. The Latin alphabet was once again exported further north, to England, where it was known as the Roman alphabet since it was passed on by the Roman Empire. The Anglo-Saxons who were controlling England were a Germanic Tribe and at that point in time they used the runic alphabet. This is when we get closer to the English language we recognize today. The Roman alphabet was combined with a few letters from the runic alphabet to create the Old English alphabet, but was not popular for writing and was seen as a lower class language, with the elites preferring to communicate in Latin. This changed in the 13th century and English started to become more and more popular. By 1600-1640 the final letter, J, was added to form the complete English alphabet that you are reading right now. I think we can all agree that all this history gives a whole new perspective to the well-known phrase "as easy as ABC!"

The word alphabet itself is derived from the first two letters of the Greek alphabet, alpha and beta, but what do really mean when we say that they are the first two letters? Why are they in that particular order? Or maybe the question should be, why are they in any particular order at all? Well, it seems like it was more an issue of practicality that the alphabet have an order, as it would make it much easier to remember than if it did not have a structure. Also, without any pre-agreed arrangement, simple things like dictionaries and encyclopaedias would not have been able to function smoothly. With regard to why they are in that particular order though, nobody seems to know. I would be more than pleased for you to contact me on the Facebook address provided in this book, should you beg to differ. What we do know is when this order was first recorded, and this was quite a long time ago, circa 1500 BC, with the Phoenicians using a recognizable order. This was not common knowledge to everyone and in fact when explaining Table Alphabeticall (seen to be the first English dictionary) in 1604, Robert Cawdrey had to actually write: "Nowe if the word, which thou art desirous to finde, begin with (a) then looke in the beginning of this Table, but if with (v) looke towards the end."

Have you ever thought about how the alphabet would look, in alphabetical order according to how the letters themselves sound? Neil deGrasse Tyson did, when he tweeted: "@neiltyson: A H R B Q D W E F L M N S X G I J K O P C T V Y U Z -- Gotta love what the alphabet looks like in alphabetical order." Therefore he means that the order would be A (A), Aich (H), Arr (R), Bee (B), Cue (Q), Dee (D), Double-you (W) and so on.

It is worthy to note that lower-case letters or minuscules were not in use simultaneously from the birth of the alphabet, and writing was done only in upper-case or majuscules. Our dual alphabet, with two different symbols for each letter, started to develop during the Middle Ages, as a result of lower-case letter being introduced through cursive writing, named Carolingian minuscule after Emperor Charlemagne. You can therefore thank him for the eventual invention of the Caps Lock button! The reason the shapes of the letters are called lower-case and upper-case are due to the fact that compositors, the humans who used to print text by manually rearranging letters to form words, used to retrieve the most commonly used letter blocks used for printing from a more accessible lower drawer or case in front of him, and the capital letters from an upper case.

So now that you know your ABCs what can you do with them? The answer is to make a pangram of course! A pangram is a phrase that uses all the letters of the alphabet at least once. The most famous pangram is probably "the quick brown fox jumps over the lazy dog", made popular by Microsoft and used when viewing or installing new fonts on our computers, but this is 35 letters long and many shorter ones do exist.

Pack my box with five dozen liquor jugs. (32 letters)

The five boxing wizards jump quickly. (31 letters)

How quickly daft jumping zebras vex. (30 letters)

Sphinx of black quartz, judge my vow. (29 letters)

Mr. Jock, TV quiz PhD, bags few lynx. (26 letters) a perfect pangram! All the letters of the alphabet are used exactly once and a perfect pangram is essentially an anagram of the alphabet itself. An anagram is a word or phrase that can be re-arranged to form a new one. Google "anagram" and look at the 'did you mean:' result (Well played Google...).

Here are some of my favourite anagrams (I have other hobbies I promise):

Elvis = Lives

Listen = Silent

Decimal Point = I'm a dot in place

William Shakespeare = I'll make a wise phrase

Debit card = Bad credit

Slot machines = Cash lost in me

Dormitory = Dirty room

Apple Inc. = Epic Plan

Christmas = Trims cash

Geologist = Go get oils

The eyes = they see

Mother-in-law = Woman Hitler

Eleven plus two = Twelve plus one

The Morse code = Here come dots

Some other interesting word plays are palindromes, words or phrases that are exactly the same word or phrase when read backwards, like:

Re-divider

Amore, Roma!

Step on no pets

Evil olive

A man, a plan, a canal...Panama!

Madam, I'm Adam

No lemon, no melon

Murder for a jar of red rum

Too bad I hid a boot

Do geese see God?

Ambigrams are words that are symmetrical when read upside down, some natural ambigrams are suns and dollop.

Finally, the semordnilap (palindromes spelled backwards!), is a word which forms a new word when spelled backwards. Some words include star (rats), drawer (rewards) and desserts (stressed). These might be useful to know when playing a game of Scrabble!

We will be looking at more word play throughout this series, but before I forget, the last anagram in the list reminded me of something. The Morse code is actually an alphabet based on the alphabet that we have been talking about, but instead of symbols, the letters are communicated by short or long bursts of light or sound.

Other famous alphabets that are based on the English alphabet but with letters being represented in a different way are the Braille alphabet (used by blind people by skimming their fingers over tiny raised dots) and the NATO Phonetic alphabet (a spelling alphabet, with its roots in aviation). Here are those alphabets reproduced in full:

International Morse Code Alphabet

The length of a dot is one unit

The length of a dash is three units

The space between parts of the same letter is one unit.

The space between letters is three units.

The space between words is seven units

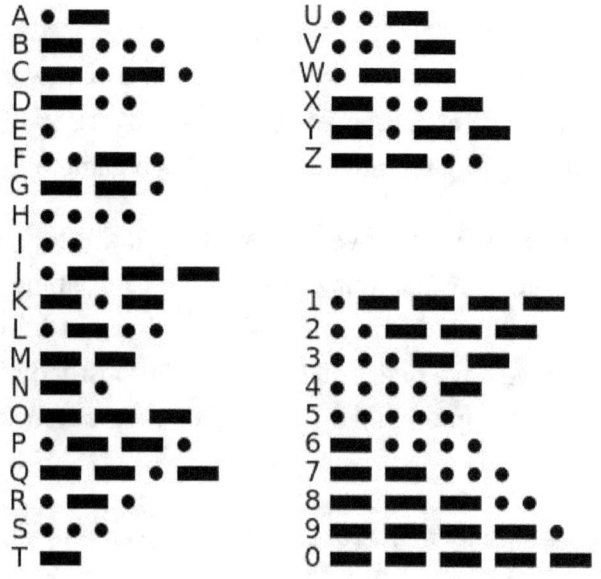

Braille Alphabet

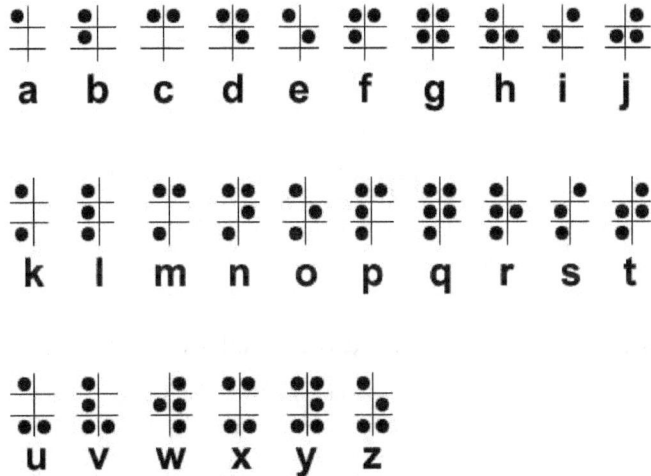

NATO Phonetic Alphabet

A = ALPHA, B = BRAVO, C = CHARLIE, D = DELTA, E = ECHO, F = FOXTROT, G = GOLF, H = HOTEL, I = INDIA, J = JULIET, K = KILO, L = LIMA, M = MIKE, N = NOVEMBER, O = OSCAR, P = PAPA, Q = QUEBEC, R = ROMEO, S = SIERRA, T = TANGO, U = UNIFORM, V = VICTOR, W = WHISKEY, X = X-RAY, Y = YANKEE, Z = ZULU

Chapter 5: Slice Of Heaven

"There's no better feeling in the world than a warm pizza box on your lap."

– Kevin James

Today I ate one of the most internationally well-known foods and also one of my favourite foods, if made right, pizza! From its hometown in Italy to some small side-street in South-East Asia, there are few places that have not learnt to make and love this dish. Not many nations can boast to have extreme success when it comes to food but Italy is one of these countries and pizza is right at the top of its food exports, with only pasta being more popular. How did this slice of heaven originate though?

Most accounts take us back to when pizza started off as flatbread in the Mediterranean, made from water and flour and seasoned with herbs. However, this result should be likened more to the modern day focaccia rather than the pizza. The pizza started to really take shape in Italy in the Middle Ages, where more modern looking pizza dough was being made and topped with olive oil, herbs and even mozzarella cheese (mozzarella di bufala) from the then recently introduced water buffalos. It was not until tomatoes were introduced to the equation that Italian pizza as we know and love it today was invented. Even though tomatoes reached Italy from the Americas by the 16th century, they only started being used in food in the late 18th century, as there was widespread belief that they were not edible and even poisonous! Pizza became especially popular in Naples, so much so, that tourists travelled there just to taste this new local cuisine, Neapolitan pizza.

Although a plethora of different types of pizza exist today, many traditionalists believe that there are really only two pure Neapolitan pizzas, the pizza marinara and the pizza Margherita. The marinara pizza is commonly confused in many countries outside of Italy as some sort of seafood pizza due to its name, and toppings such as prawns, mussels, octopus and other fishy ingredients are mistakenly included. The truth is that the proper pizza marinara is a very plain pizza indeed with no seafood whatsoever. It consists of tomatoes, olive oil, garlic and oregano and was called the pizza marinara because it was eaten by sailors when they came back after being out at sea, especially when their catch was not a very good one!

The pizza Margherita has a slightly more colourful history, if the legend is true at least. It is said that in 1889, King Umberto I and Queen Margherita were getting bored of the same French cuisine which had taken over as the food of the upper class in Italy, so they decided to invite a pizzaiolo (pizza chef), Rafaele Esposito, from Pizzeria Brandi in Naples to create different pizza recipes for them. Out of the three different pizzas that Esposito made, the pizza mozzarella was the Queen's favourite by far. This pizza was made with tomatoes, mozzarella and basil, the colours of which made up the Italian flag – red, white and green. This pizza mozzarella was quickly named the pizza Margherita in honour of the Queen and her love for it. The pizza Margherita is even recently recognized by the European Union as the real Neapolitan pizza giving it special status and imposing strict conditions to make it. To be considered authentic, a pizza Margherita must be made from a dough of highly refined type "00" wheat flour, compressed or natural yeast, water and sea salt. The tomatoes should be of the San Marzano variety in slices of 8mm or less and the mozzarella should be mozzarella di bufala Campana, that is, mozzarella made from the milk of semi-wild water buffalo living in the marshes of Lazio and Campania. By now, you should have noticed just how seriously the Italian's take their pizza!

Pizza has transformed over the years and different countries have their different takes on this famous snack, the most famous variants being the American style pizzas. The immigration of Italians to the United States brought over their love for pizza but these were only being made in Italian homes, until 1905 when Gennaro Lombardi opened the first pizzeria in America in New York City. The pizzas he made were usually thin, had a crispy crust and were very large, sometimes nearly 20 inches in diameter. Since this was too big for the average man to eat on his own, he came up with the idea of selling them by the slice, something which still happens with New York style pizza today.

After World War II the return of American soldiers from Italy, coupled with a new wave of Italian immigrants created a renewed interest in pizza in the United States. The Chicago deep-dish pizza was in fact created around this period of time by entrepreneurs Ike Sewell and his Italian partner Ric Riccardo. The creation was born by mistake when the two wanted to open a Mexican food joint but had no idea about the cuisine, so decided to settle for pizza with a twist, at their new Pizzeria Uno. It resembled a pie more than a regular pizza, with a thick crust, at least an inch high, to be able to support the large amount of toppings.

The Chicago Style pizza and the New York style pizza still battle it out to this very day and some consider them completely different products that should not even be compared. The fast food industry propelled the pizza to extreme heights in 1958 with Pizza Hut, now operating in over 100 countries, and Dominos, the first to add home delivery to the equation now with over 8000 pizzerias. Worldwide, the pizza industry is now worth around 135 billion dollars and in the United State alone it is a 40 billion dollar business. Back in Europe, the Italians try not to get too worked up by the existence of the American varieties and drive home the claim that Neapolitan pizza is the only true pizza to anyone who will listen!

Here are recipes for the two most famous Neapolitan Pizza's based on the guidelines of the *Verace Pizza Napoletana* association.

Proper Neapolitan pizza is cooked in a wood fire oven. Most homes do not have one of these readily available, so this recipe will try its best to come close to the authentic taste without the need of expensive or commercial equipment.

"We've got a wood-burning pizza oven in the garden – a luxury, I know, but it's one of the best investments I've ever made."

– Gwyneth Paltrow

Buying a pizza stone and a pizza peel would be the next best thing. A pizza stone or baking stone is placed in your regular oven and absorbs the heat from it, allowing it to simulate the effects of the very high temperatures from a wood or brick oven. The stone helps achieve a crispy crust by absorbing moisture from the dough. The pizza peel is a large, flat, shovel-like tool which is used to transfer the pizza in and out of the oven.

Ingredients for the dough (2 pizzas):

- 300g "00" wheat flour

- 1 teaspoon yeast

- 1 teaspoon sea salt

- 200ml water

Combine the flour, salt and yeast in a big bowl and mix properly. Add the water to the mixture and start to mix by hand until no dry flour remains in the bowl, creating a dough. Place damp cloth over the dough and let it rise at room temperature for a minimum of 2 hours.

After the first stage of rising, the dough should be placed onto a floured surface and divided into two equal parts, and then put into a fridge from the second stage of rising. They should be left to rise for a minimum of 6 hours but overnight would be best. After they are removed from the fridge they should be shaped into balls and left to rest at room temperature for around 2 hours.

A light layer of flour is sprinkled on the work area to keep the dough from sticking to it. Now you will be forming the base of the pizza, roughly the same size of your pizza stone or pan. With a motion from the center outwards, and with the pressure of the fingers of both hands on the dough ball, the base is turned over and around many times. By doing this, the pizzaiolo forms a disk of dough. From the center, the thickness is no more than 4 mm (plus or minus 10% is tolerated), and the border should be no greater than 1-2 cm, forming a frame or crust. The crust, known as the cornicione is one of the identifying features of the product. The base must be prepared by hand. The pizzaiolo's skill determines the movement of air in the base ensuring it moves from the center towards the periphery, thus forming the cornicione. No other method of preparation is allowed for the Verace Pizza Napoletana, and the use of a rolling pin or mechanical press is prohibited.

Place a pizza stone, if available, on the bottom rack of the oven. If a pizza stone is not available, use a pizza pan and brush it lightly with olive oil. The oven should be preheated to 250C for about 30 minutes if a pizza stone is being used, but not as long if not. Carefully lift and transfer the dough to the pizza peel (if using the pizza stone) or the pan and stretch it out into an even layer.

Since these pizzas are so simple, they rely on the highest quality ingredients.

Pizza Marinara

- Canned peeled tomatoes (70 - 100g)

- Olive oil (Virgin or Extra Virgin)

- Garlic (one clove)

- Oregano 0.5g (a pinch)

- Salt

Using a spoon, place the pressed, peeled tomatoes into the center of the pizza base, and with a spiralling motion, cover the entire surface of the base with the sauce excluding the crust (the addition or substitution of peeled tomatoes with fresh tomatoes is allowed). Remove any hard or dry sections of the clove of garlic and slice finely. Scatter the slices using the same circular motion over the tomato. Scatter a pinch of oregano in an orderly manner over the surface and add salt uniformly to the tomato sauce (if it has not been previously added). Using a traditional copper oil canister and the same spiralling motion, starting from the center and moving out, pour the olive oil over the pizza.

Pizza Margherita

- Canned peeled tomatoes (60 - 80g)

- Olive oil (Virgin or Extra Virgin)

- Mozzarella / Fior di latte (80 - 100g)

- Fresh basil (A few leaves)

- Hard cheese, grated (10 - 15g)

- Salt

Using a spoon, place the pressed, peeled tomatoes in the center of the pizza base, and with a spiralling motion, cover the entire surface of the base with the sauce excluding the crust (the addition or substitution of peeled tomatoes with fresh tomatoes is allowed). Add salt uniformly to the tomato sauce (if it has not previously been added). Spread thinly sliced strips of mozzarella or fior di latte evenly over the pizza base. Grated cheese, if added, should also be spread in a uniform manner over the base. A few basil leaves should then be placed on top of this, from the center outwards. Using a traditional copper oil canister and the same spiralling motion, starting from the center and moving out, pour the Olive oil over the pizza.

If using a pizza stone, use the pizza peel to slide the pizza onto the pizza stone in the oven rack positioned in the lower third of the oven, opening and closing the oven door as quickly as possible. If using a pizza pan, simply place the pan directly on the rack. Bake until the bottom is lightly charred and the toppings are bubbling, about 6 minutes for a chewier crust and 8 minutes for a crispier one. Although tempting, always remember to avoid opening the oven door during baking! Repeat with the remaining pizza dough and toppings. After cooking, the pizza should have the following characteristics: The tomatoes should have lost all excess water and should be dense and consistent, the mozzarella should have melted on the surface of the pizza. The basil, garlic and oregano will develop an intense aroma, and will appear brown, but not burned.

I was going to tell you some jokes about pizzas before concluding but they were too... CHEESY! Here are some anyway:

Q: Why did the man enter the pizza business?

A: He wanted to make some dough.

Q: "Waiter, will my pizza be long?"

A: "No, it will be round."

Q: What's the difference between a pizza and these pizza jokes?

A: These pizza jokes can't be topped!

Chapter 6: Brain Deception

What I if told you,

That you read

The first line wrongly.

As a young human I was always intrigued with anything that tricked my mind, like a dog fascinated by its owner pretending to throw a ball, I used to soak up anything out of the ordinary. To tell you the truth nothing has really changed and I am always eager to get fooled by something, with the sole intention of being able to learn from it and then trick other humans later on. Every book in the series will include some of these little unusual wonders. The only downside is that you can only get duped once, sort of like chicken pox... you only get it once but you can pass it on multiple times! (I actually got chicken pox twice, so maybe not the best example). Just one thing before we move on. If another human had to ever try a trick in a group, be it a magic trick, a riddle or anything else... do not ruin it for them if you know it. Same goes for a joke. Just because you know it, there is no need to get too excited. Just say that you know it and that you will not participate because you will spoil it if you do. That would garner much more respect than ruining the punchline of a joke or revealing the answer to a riddle before anyone has time to figure it out. Moving on...

Well did you read the first line wrongly? If you did, this is due to your brain expecting to read something and simply reading what it assumed would be written. Most humans would therefore read the first line incorrectly, but it's not necessarily a bad thing, it just means you are a fast reader. If you had to show the above to a young child learning to read, they would most probably read it correctly the first time since they process every word slowly.

What fruit do you like to eat in spring?

I must say I really do love oranges. Keep reading the words in the triangle above until you realize the mistake. To be fair, you may have noticed the mistake straight away given the contents of the chapter. Make somebody read it out of context and it should be a different story. It is always fascinating though to ask other humans to read it out loud and then ask them to repeat it again and again. They will usually get it wrong, not noticing the second occurrence of the word 'the' (unless they do not speak English natively or are learning to read). This, once again, is your brain expecting to see something and assuming it is there. Your brain seems to have a built in auto-correct feature, like you would find when texting on your smartphone so to speak.

Read the below paragraphs out loud, and then count the number of 'F's in each. The answers will be given right after the last passage.

FINISHED FILES ARE THE RESULT

OF YEARS OF SCIENTIFIC

STUDY COMBINED WITH THE

EXPERIENCE OF YEARS

"The necessity of training farm hands for first class farms in the fatherly handling of farm live stock is foremost in the eyes of farm owners. Since the forefathers of the farm owners trained the farm hands for first class farms in the fatherly handling of farm livestock, the farm owners feel they should carry on with the family tradition of training farm hands of first class farmers in the fatherly handling of farm live stock because they believe it is the basis of good fundamental farm management."

How many did you count in each? These passages have been doing the rounds on the Internet for quite a while, declaring that if you are able to count all of the Fs then you are some sort of genius. Unfortunately, once again, this is not the case and you would probably be able to count all the Fs on your first try if you are not a native English reader or a child still learning to read. The more fluent you are in English the more of a disadvantage you are at, unless you are a professional proof reader of course! The answers are that the first reading has 6 Fs in total, whilst the second one has 36 Fs. The reason why you probably left out so many Fs (if you did) is that you are not counting the Fs in the word 'of'. This could either be because, the word 'of' sounds like it has more of a V sound rather than the F sound that you are looking for, or simply because we are looking for more prominent words beginning with an F and the 'of' gets lost. A sort of blind spot in our brain was created.

Aoccdrnig to rscheearch at Cmabrigde Uinervtisy, it deosn't mttaer in waht oredr the ltteers in a wrod are, the olny iprmoatnt tihng is taht the frist and lsat ltteer be at the rghit pclae. The rset can be a toatl mses and you can sitll raed it wouthit a porbelm. Tihs is bcuseae the huamn mnid deos not raed ervey lteter by istlef, but the wrod as a wlohe.

You probably were able to read the previous paragraph without any problems, even though the words were jumbled up. This is also a famous paragraph that has been spread across the Internet, but while being very interesting it isn't completely true. There was no research at Cambridge University that said this but the last part could hold some truth since adult humans process words in context, rather than processing each individual letter. Your brain seems to be filling in the gaps for you. The world-wide-web even made up a fictitious trait, typoglycemia, which seems to be a mix of typo and hypoglycaemia. One could however conclude, that the words and context of the paragraph itself were relatively simple, so maybe harder words could pose greater difficulty. The humppiatopos lveos enitag a slaad at nhgit! (harder?)

What we dealt with could be called reading tricks, or maybe word blind spots? They are not illusions per se, they simply take advantage of the way our brain has been wired to read, and do not affect all people like most illusions do. Illusions can get really interesting and are successful when a human's senses have been distorted in some way or another. For the purposes of this book we shall only be giving examples of optical or visual illusions, though illusions that distort other senses, such as auditory (sound) illusions, will be discussed in later books. (If you didn't get it, the jumbled phrase was: The hippopotamus loves eating a salad at night!)

Optical illusions come in various forms and have been around from when humans began to see, with ancient man observing these optical illusions taking place naturally. When a stick was put into water for example, due to refraction it would look bent or broken when it was not. Another natural illusion is seeing the moon smaller higher up in the sky rather than at the horizon, when it is really the same distance away. Humans soon caught on to nature, and started thinking of optical illusions that they could create themselves. The first record of a human-made optical illusion is from around 500 BC, in the form of coins found on the island of Lesbos in Greece. When looking at the coins you can see two animals, goats or cows, facing each other, but when looked at in a particular way they form the face of a wolf. This sort of optical illusion is known as a cognitive illusion, and they feed off certain natural assumptions that humans think they know about the world around them. More specifically it is an ambiguous cognitive illusion, or simply an ambiguous figure, meaning that they allow for more than one interpretation of what they represent.

One of the most famous ambiguous figures is the 'Rabbit or Duck' illusion, which was first given proper attention by the American psychologist, Joseph Jastrow, and then made popular by philosopher Ludwig Wittgenstein.

Depending on how you look at the picture you could see a rabbit or a duck. A study by Brugger and Brugger in 1993 found that children who were shown this image in Easter would see it more often as a rabbit rather than as a duck. The image I included is Jastrow's own version, but the earliest known version of this drawing is from the October 1892 edition of German magazine Fliegende Blätter, where it was called "Kaninchen und Ente" ("Rabbit and Duck").

Another very popular ambiguous figure is the picture titled 'My Wife and My Mother-in-Law'.

The creation of the image is usually incorrectly attributed to W.E. Hill, a British cartoonist who published the picture in an American magazine in 1915. The earliest traces of this illusion however, go back to an uncredited German postcard from 1888 which is nearly identical to Hill's version and various others before his, meaning that he must have copied it from one of them. The image was made popular in the psychology community by R.W. Leeper (in 1935) and E.G. Boring (in 1942), and became known as the Boring figure. In this illusion you can either see a young lady (wife) looking over her shoulder or an older woman (mother-in-law) looking straight ahead, depending on how you look at it. The older woman's nose is the young lady's chin. As with most ambiguous illusions, it may take time to see both interpretations, but once you do, you cannot "unsee" one of them. This image is really true to life, as once you meet your mother-in-law, you cannot unmeet her! (Just joking J!)

Chapter 7: Fingers Crossed!

Today a human wished me "Good luck!" right before I set off to perform a particular task. Although I am not a very superstitious person myself, I cannot deny that luck is a common theme in our world. Luck is indeed an interesting concept that we have created and I would say that it came about mainly due to the fact that humans love to overthink everything about their lives and try to come up with reasons for events that really do not require any explanation at all. This is not necessarily such a bad thing, and being curious as to why something has happened is one of the most common of human traits. Giving meaning to outcomes is a means of getting some sort of closure perhaps. Is it good luck that some children are born in stable areas and others in countries ravaged by war? Is it good luck when you are walking and find money on the floor? Accepting that certain things in life are either simply random or determined solely by our actions is probably a boring stance to take for most humans, hence why we have created superstitions.

We have come up with elaborate ways that we believe would change our luck from bad to good and try to avoid any situations that we believe would change our luck from good to bad. Good luck superstitions have existed in many different cultures for thousands of years, and range from performing an action, saying particular words, or carrying around an object like a charm or amulet. Crossing one's fingers for example dates back to the early Christians protecting themselves against evil by forming a cross with their fingers if they did not have a physical cross handy. In typical 21st century fashion, we have now shortened the action to just words when we say "fingers crossed!" Do not cross your fingers in Vietnam though, as this is highly offensive!

"See a penny and pick it up, all the day you'll have good luck. See a penny and let it lay, bad luck you'll have all the day."

The superstition of picking a coin up from the ground bringing good luck has been around since coins started becoming commonplace, and similar superstitions existed before this with other types of metal objects. This was because metal was seen as a gift from the gods to protect us against evil, and refusing a gift that they clearly gave you (why else would it be on the floor?) would result in bad luck. Coins also signify wealth and power, so picking these up and carrying them on you would attract more of the same. Variations exist where you should only pick up a coin from the ground if it is heads up for you to receive the blessings or you could pass it on to somebody else for the luck to be bestowed upon them instead, but you should keep on walking if it is tails up. This is probably representing the constant battle between good and evil that has been present from the beginning of time. There is no denying that picking up coins would still make one wealthier whatever the size of the coin as every little counts, so there is no point in not picking one up. Even if you are not superstitious yourself, why not make a fellow human's day luckier and leave a coin on the ground (head ups of course!) for them to find and pick up.

One of the most common good luck charms, and in my opinion one of strangest, is the lucky rabbit's foot. I could never quite get to terms with the idea of carrying a dead animals severed body part around, but I guess if other humans do this, it must make sense right? This tradition goes back to around 600 BC, with the Celts using them for protection, as they believed that since these animals lived underground they were close to the underworld and in turn, the gods and spirits. The importance of the rabbit foot was introduced to America however by the African-American community, with the folk-magic practice of hoodoo. When their magic called for using witches' bones, rabbit parts were often used instead. We all know that witches in human form are pretty difficult to get hold of, but fortunately (or unfortunately for the rabbit) they are believed to change their form into that of a rabbit quite often! The rabbit foot then started to become more mainstream, with it being sold in America as a good luck charm as protection against evil. Many variations existed as to how the foot had to be acquired but the most prominent was that the foot had to be the back left foot of a rabbit that was killed at a cemetery during the night, preferably on Friday the 13th of course! Other variations say that the little animals must be killed during a specific phase of the moon by none other than… a cross-eyed man. No matter what your beliefs are on this particular superstition, we can probably all agree that with all the luck rabbits bring, the poor creatures are not the luckiest of animals themselves!

Thankfully, a horse's foot has never been considered lucky (can you imagine the keychain?), but its shoe has a whole different story. Horseshoes have been lucky for a long time, and the fact that they are made of metal, just like coins, made it easier for them to be considered as such. Iron in particular was considered to be even more magical as it could withstand tremendous amounts of heat and was much stronger than any other metal at the time. To build even further upon the magical properties of the horseshoe, a legend exists involving Saint Dunstan. Before he was the Archbishop of Canterbury, Dunstan worked as a blacksmith, and on one particular day the Devil just happened to walk into his shop (as the Devil does...) and asked him to put horseshoes on his horse. Dunstan immediately recognized the Devil (as one would) but did not let on to this fact, and instead hammered the horseshoe into the Devil's hoof. The Devil, was in great agony, and Dunstan only removed the horseshoe after he made the Devil promise not to ever enter a house which had a horseshoe nailed to it. The most common way to hang a horseshoe is in the upright direction (like a U) and preferably with 7 nails (as 7 was always a lucky number), with most believers saying that doing otherwise would allow your luck to escape, however as with all superstitions there is no universal rule (I wonder why!).

Other animals that unluckily for them bring luck for humans are the chicken, turkey, goose and other fowl, whose wishbone or *furcula* is said to bring about good fortune. Earliest mentions of this superstition find that any person holding this part of the animal's chest was able to think hard about what they desired and their thoughts would come to fruition quicker, and the name *merrythought* was in use before wishbone precisely for this reason. During the late 17th century the tradition of two humans holding this bone and tugging at it with the aim of pulling away the biggest part developed. The person who broke off the bigger part was able to make a wish, hence the term wishbone which came about in the late 19th century. The phrase "to get a lucky break" in fact originated from this practice.

Among a long list of other creatures believed to bring luck, this time with a figurine or mere sighting being enough, are the elephant, tortoise and frog. The belief in these animals' lucky qualities originated from Asia but soon spread to different corners of the world. The elephant for example was always a symbol of good fortune in Asia but quickly became important in many other cultures were it was understood to represent power and wisdom. The most popular tradition is to have an elephant figurine, preferably with the trunk up, facing the front door of a house, to bestow good luck upon the owner. In fact these ornaments are one of the most popular souvenirs that one takes back home with them after visiting Asia. The tortoise primarily represents longevity, as it lives on average between 80 to 150 years, with Jonathan, a Seychelles giant tortoise living on the island of Saint Helena, hatched in 1832 and still going strong at 184 years of age as I write this. A figurine of a tortoise placed on coins is also said to bring the owner wealth apart from longevity. Frogs and toads have often been a sign of good luck in many cultures throughout history. Since these amphibians come out when the spring season is just starting they have come to represent new beginnings and due to their many biological changes, they are also seen as a symbol of change and transformation. The most famous figurine is Jin Chan, the Chinese three-legged money toad, which helps the owner to attract good fortune, specifically wealth, and protect against any bad luck.

A peculiar lucky charm that only stopped being popular in the 19th century, is associated with the word *abracadabra*. We all probably know this word from magicians waving their wands, but the history of this word goes much further back than that. Records of this charm's origins go as far back as the 2nd century AD, when a certain sage Sammonicus writes about how to use it correctly. It was said that if you write the word abracadabra 11 times on a piece of paper, removing the last letter of the word every time you write it, to form a sort of cone-shape, you would be protected against evil and cured of any diseases if you carried this around with you. (Sounds legit!)

ABRACADABRA

ABRACADABR

ABRACADAB

ABRACADA

ABRACAD

ABRACA

ABRAC

ABRA

ABR

AB

A

My personal favourite lucky charm was always the four-leaf clover, possibly due to my love for all things Irish (especially my Irish mother!). However, I later found out that the origins of the four-leaf clover came about way before it became associated with the Irish, and in fact Christian legend holds that Eve was holding one when she was expelled from the Garden of Eden (maybe it wasn't so lucky back then!). Irish are said to be the luckiest people around, after all they have the luck of the Irish. However some theories say that the term 'luck of the Irish' was intended to mean anything but good luck, and really meant bad luck due to the many consecutive hardships that the Irish were facing. Other theories hold that many people looked upon the Irish who immigrated to America and became successful, as simply being lucky rather than it being due to their hard work. The four-leaf clover is not one in a million, but actually around 1 in 10,000 clovers have 4 leaves, with the most common having 3 leaves (shamrock). In Irish lore, each of the four leaves represents a certain virtue, being faith, hope, love and the fourth leaf representing luck. We should leave the number of leaves at 4 though, as even though a 5 leaf clover can occur, the Irish believe that instead of being even luckier it is actually bad luck!

When it comes to luck I think that some people give too much importance to it, rather than focusing on doing those things that will definitely help achieve the results they want. I tend to agree with Brian Tracy who said: "I've found that luck is quite predictable. If you want more luck, take more chances. Be more active. Show up more often." He is basically saying that you cannot just sit and do nothing and expect good luck to come your way, you need to do something about it. Receiving good luck has also been used as a cover for certain misfortunes. The Italians have a saying "sposa bagnata, sposa fortunata" which means, a rainy wedding is a lucky one. I think what they are really trying to do though is put the couple at ease, since the outcome is going to be lucky either way. If it doesn't rain you are lucky because you can enjoy the wedding but if it does rain you have this good luck bestowed upon you, a win-win situation. This reminds me of when I found out that a friend of mine had a bad accident and it was said that it was very lucky that she didn't die, I thought to myself, if she were very lucky she would not have been involved in that accident in the first place! Now that we have had a look at some lucky superstitions in this chapter, you can read about some unlucky ones that humans came up with over the years, later on in this book, in the chapter with the alleged unlucky number!

Chapter 8: That's Nuts!

Today I bought a box of mixed nuts. Amongst other things it contained peanuts, which I remember being told as a child were not really nuts. I wondered if any of the other so-called nuts in the mixture had a similar story to that of peanuts, and to my surprise this was indeed the case. Many of the "nuts" that we eat are not nuts at all. What I also realized was that I did not know how to define a nut, and maybe that is where I should start. In botany, a nut in its true form is a pod with a dry, hard outer shell that contains both the fruit and the seed, and where the fruit does not open to release this seed. So a nut is essentially a dry, hard fruit in which the seed can be found inside. Commercially popular true nuts that we eat include hazelnuts, pecan nuts and chestnuts. The rest of the commercially available "nuts" are not nuts at all, and these include: almonds, pistachios, walnuts, peanuts, Brazil nuts, macadamia nuts, pine nuts and cashew nuts. Edible "nuts" whether true nuts or not can be grouped in the catch-all term of culinary nuts.

Almonds are very popular, having actually recently overtaken peanuts to claim the top spot when it comes to culinary nut consumption in the USA, and it is California which produces 80% of the world's almonds in this 4 billion dollar industry. Almonds are actually being blamed for California droughts, due to their very water thirsty nature, needing around a gallon (nearly 4 litres) of water to produce one almond. Almonds are not true nuts but are actually seeds from the fruit of the almond tree. Fruits like these, with a fleshy outer layer encasing a shell with a seed inside, are called drupes. Some commonly eaten drupes include peaches, plums, cherries and olives, but the seed inside is not edible. In the case of almonds and other drupe seeds such as pistachios and walnuts, they are seeds that just happen to be edible too.

Peanuts are probably the most famous culinary nuts and they are in fact legumes and not true nuts, as they are plants which grow seeds inside pods (like peas). Peanuts grow in quite a unique way. The peanut seeds actually start flowering above ground and then due to their increasing weight start drooping towards the ground, where they then burrow and mature. It is easy to tell that peanuts are not really nuts as true nuts grow on trees, whereas peanuts would have to be pulled from the ground during harvest time. The main producers of peanuts are India and China with the USA coming in third place. Nearly all peanuts produced in the USA are used to make peanut butter, a mixture that by law requires at least 90% peanuts.

Brazil nuts and macadamia nuts are angiosperm seeds and form inside an enclosure, that of a larger fruit, whereas pine nuts (the most common being the stone pine nut, an essential ingredient in pesto) are gymnosperm seeds and do not develop in an enclosure. I only recently just put two and two together and realized that pine nuts are actually found in pine cones. They are so expensive because they take a lot of man power to harvest since the seeds usually have to be handpicked from between the scales of the pine cone. Brazil nuts are mostly produced in Bolivia rather than Brazil, and they are not called Brazil nuts in Brazil but chestnuts. Brazil nuts grow high up in trees in round heavy wooden capsules and are released when the enclosure falls from the tree. Macadamia nuts are also found inside a hard enclosure containing one or two of these white creamy seeds. The largest Macadamia producer in the world is currently South Africa, which only just recently took the lead from Australia, which had surpassed the USA (specifically Hawaii) in the 1960s.

Perhaps the most interesting of these culinary nuts is the cashew nut. Ironically, cashew nuts, not Brazil nuts, originated in Brazil! Cashew nuts were once eaten in small portions due to their rarity but now large packets can be purchased for relatively cheap from your local supermarket. The ever increasing popularity of the cashew nut fuels its production, which is anything but an easy task. They are never sold in their shell due to the highly acidic nature of this layer, which can burn human skin. Cashew nut production has lately drawn controversy, with Time magazine labelling the industry "blood cashews", due to the fact that Vietnamese exports (the largest cashew nut producer) have been marred with reports of forced and cheap labour.

The cashew nut is in fact really a seed of a fruit known as the cashew apple. However, rather than the seed developing inside like in drupes, a single cashew nut hangs from the bottom of each fruit, known as an accessory fruit. See a picture of a cashew apple hanging from a tree below, it is quite impressive. The cashew apple itself is edible and very tasty, but it is so highly perishable (spoiling in around 24 hours), that it is only sold in the areas that it is grown and not exported. So remember, next time you reach for a nut from that box of mixed nuts, first of all remember that you are probably not eating a true nut at all and second, appreciate all the time and work it took from different corners of the earth just to make this mixture for you!

Chapter 9: It's A Kind Of Magic!

This card trick does not require any prior preparation of the pack and relies more on deception of the audience than anything else. You will first have to bring out a pack of normal playing cards and give them a good shuffle. Then, starting from the top card, form a 4 x 4 grid horizontally, left to right, top to bottom (the fact that you are doing this horizontally is important). If there are too many similar cards in the same row or column replace them with different cards and simply tell the audience that you do not want to confuse them. You should now have 16 cards in a 4 x 4 grid.

Now tell your audience (this is usually better with one human at a time by the way!) to choose one card and to remember it without revealing what they have chosen. Once they have memorized their card, ask them what row it's in, out of the 4 rows in front of them. Let's say they choose Row 2 (remember Ace of Hearts – 4 of Hearts – 10 of Clubs – Queen of Diamonds). Memorize that sequence and start collecting the cards one by one, however this time vertically and not horizontally. So pick up the first card from Row 1, then the first card from Row 2 (which goes on top of the first card from Row 1) and so on. When you have all the cards in your hand start dealing from the top of the pack in a horizontal manner (important), left to right, top to bottom, to form another 4 x 4 grid. The row they chose now appears as a column, in this case, column 3.

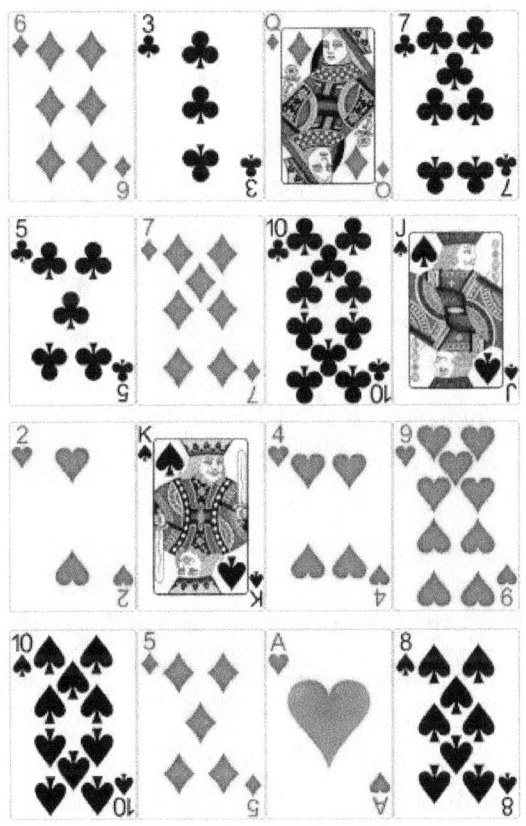

You should now ask them if they still see their card, and you could act a bit surprised if they say that they do (just a bit of misdirection). Ask them what row it is in again. Let's say they choose Row 2 again. You now know that their card is the 10 of clubs. Start to collect the cards again, it does not matter how you collect them but since you collected them vertically before you could continue with this for consistency's sake. The most important thing here is to remember where their card is when you collect all the cards. You will get used to this the more and more you perform the trick. What I usually do is collect the cards to the top of the pack until I get to their card, then continue collecting the cards but place them at the bottom of the pack, this way I would know that their card is the top card of the pack. If you do this fast enough they will not notice the change. Alternatively, once you get to their card, keep on collecting as normal but count how many cards have gone on top of their card. In our example it would be 6 cards on top of theirs, as their card would be the 10th card picked up.

Next you will arrange the cards face down (important) into four groups of 4. You can do this haphazardly drawing some cards from the top of the pack and some cards from the bottom, as long as you remember where their card is. In this example their card is the first card in the bottom left group.

Tell them to choose any two groups from the four choices in front of them, do not tell them why. Now comes the deceptive part. The aim of this part of the trick is for them to eventually be left with just their card, so we do not want to discard their card at any point. If they choose two groups that DO NOT include their card simply discard both those groups into a pile, however if they choose two groups, one of which contains their card, you would need to discard the two groups that they DID NOT select. In our example they choose the top groups, so we would need to discard both of these, since their card is in the bottom left group.

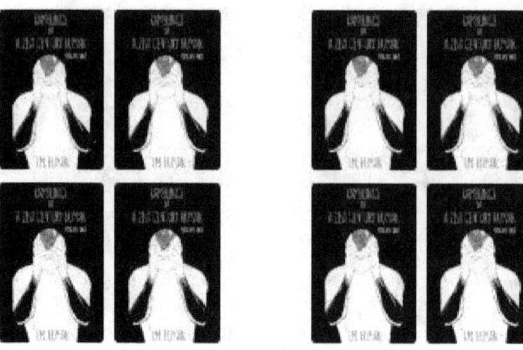

Now we are left with two groups, repeat the process and ask them to choose any one of the two groups. If they choose the group that does not contain their card, discard it. If they choose the group that contains their card, discard the other group instead.

Now you are left with one group. Repeat the process this time asking them to choose any two cards. You guessed it... if they choose two cards that do not include their card, discard them, if the two card contains their card, then discard the other two cards.

Two cards left! This is where the "magic" happens and one of these cards is definitely their card. Simply tell them to point at any card. Ideally they point at their card (it's a 50% chance). If they do not point at their card tell them to discard the card they pointed at and to turn over the card that is remaining. If they point at their card tell them to turn it over. They should be amazed. You cannot do this too many times with the same audience, as eventually they might catch on to the fact that you are not consistent with your discarding of groups and cards, but it is a quick trick that can be easily set up without sleight of hand or preparation. Very useful to impress humans at a family event or even to win a few bets at a bar!

Chapter 10: And?

We earlier discussed the already well known fact that the English alphabet consists of 26 letters, but this was not always the case until quite recently. In fact, a certain famous symbol held the prestigious title of being the 27th letter of the alphabet (although not representing a sound of speech) and it can still be seen throughout the world today. If you had to look at a standard computer keyboard you would see it quietly resting on top of the number 7, a very beautiful symbol indeed. The '&' sign is known as the ampersand and is short for 'and'. Its first origins can be found in the commonly used word 'et' which means 'and' in Latin. A shorthand for the word 'et' reminiscent of the ampersand was created by Marcus Tullius Tiro and recorded in his Tironian Notes (circa 63 BC). With enough imagination you will notice that the letters 'e' and 't' combined (et) do in fact resemble the curvy '&' symbol! The Tironian 'et' eventually lost its popularity and stopped being used almost in its entirety, yet we can still see it today in Ireland, were it used in Gaelic signs.

It must be pointed out that although there is a resemblance in the shorthand Tironian 'et' and &, they are two totally different symbols developing separately. The evolution of the ampersand as a separate symbol can be traced back to the 1st century AD, around 100 years after Tiro's Tironian Notes, and a graffiti on a wall in Pompeii dating back to at least 79 AD (when the volcano Mount Vesuvius erupted and destroyed the city of Pompeii) serves to prove this. This ampersand was quite a primitive one though, and we would need to fast forward to the 9th century AD, to the Carolignian cursive version of the ampersand, to see the version of the logogram that we know and love (is that too strong?) today.

By the early 19th century, the ampersand was a part of everyday life, the last letter of the alphabet, and an essential block for a printer. Johannes Gutenberg, the inventor of the first printing press, included both standard and italic versions in his original press models that first appeared in 1440. It was quite a long time after the symbol was created though, that the name ampersand was given to it, and the story behind the name of the symbol is quite a curious one. Some sources attribute the surnames of humans who supposedly made it popular, which would prefix the word 'and', such surnames as Amper or Ampere (to make Amper's and or Ampere's and), but this is not correct. The origin of the name came about due to spelling in the middle ages being taught syllable by syllable as opposed to letter by letter. Problems came about when a letter was also a word when looked at by itself, such as the preposition 'a' and the personal pronoun 'i', as students would spell the word letter by letter, and then say the word itself. Since saying a − a or i − i would be unclear, they needed to separate it with something, and this is how 'per se' (which means 'on its own' in Latin) came to be used. Students would therefore spell 'a' as 'a per se a'.

When reciting the 27-letter alphabet a situation arose where, since the '&' sign was short for the word 'and', the reciting of the alphabet would end in: W, X, Y, Z and &. To avoid confusion, students began to insert 'per se' in between both of the ands. Therefore, alphabet recitals used to end with: W, X, Y, Z and per se and. Say those last 4 words fast a couple of times. This is what eventually happened over time. Students reciting the alphabet over and over again began to form a new word and the original words lost their meaning, forming the word ampersand instead. When this occurs it is known as a mondegreen, meaning that a new word or meaning is formed due to the mishearing or mispronunciation of another word or phrase. The word mondegreen itself started off as a mondegreen, and was coined by writer Sylvia Wright, who misheard a song containing the lyrics "laid him on the green" as "Lady Mondegreene". This particular mondegreen word survived, and ampersand made it to the dictionary by 1837. We have a lot of bored students repetitively reciting the alphabet to thank for the existence of this word!

One of the earliest known children's alphabet rhymes from the 18th century, known as the Apple Pie ABC rhyme went something like this (notice that the I and U are missing, as back then J and V were used interchangeably with these letters):

"A was an apple pie, B bit it, C cut it, D dealt it, E eat it, F fought for it, G got it, H had it, J joined it, K kept it, L longed for it, M mourned for it, N nodded at it, O opened it, P peeped in it, Q quartered it, R ran for it, S stole it, T took it, V viewed it, W wanted it, X, Y, Z, and Ampersand... all wished for a piece in hand!"

We can still see the ampersand being used today all over the place, even though it had been removed from the alphabet, it is still a very much used symbol. In writing in can be a bit tricky to actually reproduce the '&' sign perfectly, so many humans simply draw a backward 3 with a line going through it. Generally speaking the word 'and' and the logogram '&' can be used interchangeably, but there are cases where there are subtle differences between the two. For example the Writers Guild of America (WGA) states that when crediting writers or screenplay authors, when names are joined with the word 'and' it signifies that the writers did not work together when writing. However when names are joined with the ampersand symbol, it means that they wrote together or formed part of a team. Maybe we would like to think that the '&' sign can subtly imply a closer bond between the words that they are joining, many wedding invitations are a great example of this!

One of my favourite modern day uses of the ampersand, comes from a 2001 T-shirt design by designers Experimental Jetset for the Japanese t-shirt label 2K/Gingham. In their original design they listed the names of the members of The Beatles under each other separated by an ampersand, so "John & Paul & Ringo & George." They later made Rolling Stones (Keith & Mick & Bill & Charlie & Brian.) and Ramones versions (Joey & DeeDee & Johnny & Tommy.) This design became one of the most popular T-shirt designs of the 21st century and has been copied and parodied to include countless different combinations of names, all because of the simple inclusion of the striking ampersand. The Internet cooking sensation Epic Meal Time came out with a great parody of the design with their best-selling "BaconStrips & BaconStrips & BaconStrips & BaconStrips & BaconStrips." T-shirt.

Here are some of the most famous brands that have made the ampersand a part of their identity:

M&Ms: Did anybody ever refer to these bite size chocolates as M and Ms? The ampersand is definitely an essential part of the branding here. The Ms actually stand for the names of the owners of the then M&M company; Forrest Mars, the son of the owner of the Mars Company, the same one that produced the Mars bar (I always thought it was named after the planet...) and Bruce Murrie, the son of the president of Hershey Chocolate. Quite a sweet (get it?) partnership going on there!

J&B Blended Scotch Whiskey: J&B, the 2nd best-selling blended scotch whiskey after Johnnie Walker, is actually short for Justerini & Brooks.

H&M: Swedish multinational clothing company, short for Hennes & Mauritz.

M&S or Marks & Spencer: British multinational retailers, established in 1884 by Michael Marks and Thomas Spencer.

D&G or Dolce & Gabbana: Italian luxury brand founded in 1985 by Italian designers Domenico Dolce and Stefano Gabbana.

Ben & Jerry's: Famous ice-cream brand founded by childhood friends Ben Cohen and Jerry Greenfield.

AT&T: The American Telephone and Telegraph Company.

Black & Decker: This power tool company was founded in 1910 by Samuel Duncan Black and Alonzo Decker. They have recently dropped the ampersand from their identity and replaced it with a plus sign, Black + Decker, apparently in a bid to look more minimalistic.

Can you think of any other companies or brands that have the ampersand as a part of their image?

Chapter 11: Yo Mama!

If we had to go back in time and take a look at the first maternal insult ever recorded, we would have to go back 3500 years to circa 1500 BC to a phrase written on a tablet (a stone tablet...) by a Babylonian student. It goes something like "of your mother is by the one who has intercourse with her." Whilst incomplete, this can still be seen as the first proof of humans insulting loved ones rather than directly insulting a fellow human.

Insults like these prey on one's filial piety, the respect one has for their parents and elders. Some more complete and coherent maternal insults can be found in the 1600s by Shakespeare in his play "Titus Andronicus", where this happens:

Demetrius: "Villain, what hast thou done?"

Aaron: "That which thou canst not undo."

Chiron: "Thou hast undone our mother."

Aaron: "Villain, I have done thy mother."

In another Shakespearean play "Timon of Athens", Apemantus compares a painter's mother to a dog in this great comeback:

Painter: "Y'are a dog."

Apemantus: "Thy mother's of my generation. What's she, if I be a dog?"

Although maternal insult jokes in the form we recognize today originated and became famous in the 1990s, it was in the 19th century in the time of slavery that turn-based insults became the norm in African-American communities. This was known as The Dozens. Some theories hold that this was practiced in order for lower slaves to vent against the higher ranked slaves without physical altercations. Other theories say it was not a game at all, but practice for the slaves to endure the insults from their masters. Topics used in The Dozens were the receiver's negative traits, ugliness, stupidity, poorness and of course the same remarks against the receiver's relatives, especially mothers, presumably because they were closer to the opponent's heart.

Yo Mama! jokes as we know them today became popular in their distinct form in the 1990s, once again through black culture, but this time through more modern mediums such as rap music and hip-hop lyrics on the radio and TV. The word mama has become such a general term that the actual mothers of the opponents are probably not even directly imagined and is not meant literally, but come to represent some fictional character with these negative traits. Therefore, nowadays these jokes are not meant to be offensive to anyone in any shape or form. Here are some of the more popular Yo Mama jokes:

Yo mama so ugly, her portraits hang themselves!

Yo mama so ugly, she makes blind children cry!

Yo mama so ugly, when she joined an ugly contest they said, "Sorry, no professionals!"

Yo mama so ugly, she made the onions cry!

Yo mama so ugly, they pay her to put her clothes ON at strip clubs!

Yo mama so ugly, she went into a haunted house, and came out with a job application!

Yo mama so ugly, when she walks into a bank, they turn off the surveillance cameras!

Yo mama so ugly, she tried to take a bath and the water jumped out!

Yo mama so ugly, she made a happy meal... sad!

Yo mama so fat, she went out in high heels and struck oil!

Yo mama so fat, she left the house in high heels and when she got back, they were flip-flops!

Yo mama so fat, when she walked out onto the pier, people tried to board her!

Yo mama so fat, she's on both sides of the family!

Yo mama so fat, she got pushed back into the ocean by members of Greenpeace!

Yo mama so fat, Dracula bit her neck and got diabetes!

Yo mama so fat, when she fell in love, she broke it!

Yo mama so fat, she wears a watch on both wrists... one for each time zone!

Yo mama so fat, she had to go to Sea World to get baptized!

Yo mama so fat, she wore a yellow raincoat and people yelled taxi!

Yo mama so fat, she wore a yellow raincoat and children thought they missed their school bus!

Yo mama so fat, she broke your family tree!

Yo mama so fat, she has more rolls than a bakery!

Yo mama so fat, that when she steps on a weighing scale it says: to be continued.

Yo mama so fat, the only letters she knows in the alphabet are K.F.C!

Yo mama so fat, she sat on an iPhone and it turned into an iPad!

Yo mama so fat, she's got her own area code!

Yo mama so fat, she ate a whole Pizza... Hut!

Yo mama so fat, when she goes camping, the bears have to hide THEIR food!

Yo mama so fat, I swerved to miss her and ran out of gas!

Yo mama so old and fat, that when God said "Let there be Light", he told her to move out of the way!

Yo mama so old, the candles cost more than the birthday cake!

Yo mama so old, she sat next to Jesus in school!

Yo mama so old, she knew the Burger King when he was still a prince!

Yo mama so old, when she was young, rainbows were black and white!

Yo mama so old, when she was in school there was no history class!

Yo mama so old, she has Adam and Eve's autographs!

Yo mama so old, she has a picture of Moses in her school yearbook!

Yo mama so stupid, she studied for her blood test!

Yo mama so stupid, she got fired from the M&Ms factory for throwing away all the W's!

Yo mama so stupid, she got hit by a parked car!

Yo mama so stupid, when the computer said "Press any key to continue", she couldn't find the "Any" key!

Yo mama so stupid, she studied for her pregnancy test!

Yo mama so stupid, she went to the dentist to get Bluetooth!

Yo mama so stupid, she got locked in a grocery store and starved!

Yo mama so poor, she washes the paper plates!

Yo mama so poor, she can't even pay attention!

Yo mama so poor, she eats cereal with a fork just to save on milk!

Chapter 12: Until I Am Measured, I Am Not Known. Yet How You Miss Me, When I Have Flown!

What time is it? A question that is asked countless times a day, but is it ever really answered correctly? Sure, we can say it is twenty minutes past nine in the morning, or when asked for the date we can say it is the 27th of October, but do these answers really mean anything? The truth is that these answers are only relevant in the context of time that we, as humans, have created, and these systems were put in place simply to allow us to live an easier life. We must realize that measuring time is a man-made concept. As I am writing this chapter, it is the year 2016 in the Gregorian calendar, and the year 1437 in the Islamic calendar and the year 4713 in the Chinese calendar! The Gregorian calendar is the calendar the majority of the world uses today, although other calendars are sometimes used for social and religious reasons.

The most commonly used measurement devices that humans have created to track time are the calendar and the clock. To be fair, the term measurement device should be used very loosely. Let us say you wake up in a room alone, you have lost your memory and you do not know where you are or what day it is. For the sake of this argument, and for the more pedantic reader, this room has no windows! You find a measuring tape, a weighing scale, a thermometer, a compass, a clock and a calendar in this room. With the measuring tape you can accurately measure the room, and yourself. The weighing scale will help you find out how much you weigh or the weight of any object around you. The temperature in the room can be determined with the thermometer and you can find out where north is by using the compass. However, the clock and the calendar are relatively useless in your predicament. You cannot tell if the clock is telling the right time because you need to know the correct time to begin using it and similarly the calendar is unusable because without having a reference point to start with, you cannot calculate the date. There is no outside force that will magically update these devices, it is truly a man-made concept. These tools have never really measured time, they just define it.

Humans could have chosen a system of telling the time from an infinite number of possibilities and this would have been known as the time today, still not a true measure of time but it would represent our notion of the concept of time in some way or another. Time in its simplest form can be thought of in the sense of past, present and future. They are constantly changing. The chapter you are reading now is being read in the present. The previous one was read in the past and the next one will be read in the future. Even the last sentence that you just read, which was the present previously, has now become the past. Fortunately for us, some humans with a lot of time on their hands (pun?) devised standard ways for all of this to make sense to us, by creating measurements such as years, months, weeks, days, hours, minutes and seconds.

The calendar was invented to keep track of years, months, weeks and days. By using it properly you can tell what day it is today, how many weeks left for a particular event and how many years ago something happened. The basis for many of the first calendars such as the Greeks, Chinese and Babylonians was the moon, and that is why they were called lunar calendars. Lunar calendars would take into account the phases of the moon and more specifically, the time taken for a new moon to become a new moon.

The first proper steps to what would become the calendar we use nowadays would come in the form of the Roman calendar, which was heavily based on the Greek lunar calendar. King Romulus, the first king of Rome, is said to have created this calendar, but it seems that early Romans would credit Romulus with certain inventions when the true originator was not known. The calendar of Romulus had 10 months and started in Martius (our March). The names of the months were: Martius (March), Aprilis (April), Maius (May), Iunius (June), Quintilis, Sextilis, September, October, November and December. Familiar Right? Martius was the beginning of the year and the time when soldiers would begin war so it was named after the God of war, Mars. Aprilis came from the word meaning 'to open' (aperio), Maius was named after Maia who symbolized growth and Iunius came about from iunior, meaning younger. The rest of the months derived from the Latin words for numbers, five through to ten, since they were the 5th to 10th months on the calendar.

The 12 month calendar was formed when the next, and second king of Rome, Numa Pompilius, added Ianuarius (January) and Februarius (February) to the equation because the previous calendar was not aligning with the seasons correctly. Ianuarius was named after Janus, God of beginnings, whereas Februarius was named after the Roman festival of purification, Februa. The year now had 355 days with the 12 month calendar, as opposed to 304 days in the previous 10 month calendar, but was still flawed. Numa Pompilius even tried to make the calendar align to the seasons by adding an extra month, known as intercalaris or Mercedonius, in leap years.

It was not until Julius Ceasar came along, that this lunar calendar was replaced with a solar calendar in 45 BC, trying to mimic the exact time it takes Earth to complete the orbit around the sun, with 365 days, 12 months and with every 4th year being a leap year. The month Quintilis, was changed to Iulius (July) by Mark Anthony, to honour Julius Ceasar and his successor Augustus later renamed the month Sextilis to Augustus (August), to honour himself, thus completing the name of the months that we use today. The Julian calendar unfortunately still proved to be inaccurate due to the system in which it calculated leap years, every 4th year without exception, and as a result introduced an extra day every 128 years. The solution to this problem arrived with the Gregorian calendar in the late 15th century.

The Gregorian calendar is the calendar that most of the world uses today and this amended version of the Julian calendar was proposed by Italian astronomer Aloysius Lilius and introduced by Pope Gregory XIII in 1582. It proposed that we build upon the leap year every 4 years like in the Julian calendar, but exclude leap years if the year was a century year (divisible by 100), like the year 1900. The exception to the rule was when the century year was divisible by 400, like the year 2000, therefore making it a leap year. This essentially excluded 3 leap years every 4 centuries, making it significantly more accurate. It still isn't completely perfect though, as we are adding an extra 27 seconds per year or a day every 3236 years. Solutions to this problem were also proposed, with astronomer John Herschel suggesting we exclude every year divisible by 4000 from being a leap year, but this has not been implemented yet.

Although the Gregorian calendar was first introduced in 1582, it took more than 300 years for the whole word to adapt to it, with some countries such as Greece and Turkey adopting it in 1923 and 1927 respectively. Even the United States took long to conform to this, with most areas adopting the system in 1752. That is why, in fact, some influential humans of the time have two birthdays, one based on the Julian calendar and one on the Gregorian. George Washington was born on both February 22nd 1732 and February 11th 1731, depending on which calendar you were following!

Some attempts to change the calendar year did indeed take place, with France opting to change the Gregorian calendar for a new calendar as a way of starting afresh, thus the French Revolutionary calendar or the French Republican calendar came to be in the late 18th century. This calendar still had 365 days in the year, since nothing, not even the French revolution could change the time it takes the Earth to orbit around the sun! Therefore, the difference was to be in how the year was divided. The 7-day week was replaced by a 10-day week called a décade, and there were 3 décades in each of the 12 months. The remaining 5 days (or 6 days in leap years) were called supplementary days.

New names for the months and days of the week also needed to be invented for this Revolutionary calendar, so poet Fabre d'Eglantine was appointed to breathe new life into these. The names of the days were simply the number of that particular day in the week, so there was: *primidi (first day), duodi (second day), tridi (third day), quartidi (fourth day), quintidi (fifth day), sextidi (sixth day), septidi (seventh day), octidi (eight day), nonidi (ninth day) and décadi (tenth day).* Not too creative in my opinion, however the names of the months and individual days (yes, every single day had a different name) surely made up for this. The twelve months were aptly named after natural occurrences that happened around the same time of the month itself and they were called: *Vendémiaire (grape harvest month), Brumaire (fog month), Frimaire (frost month), Nivôse (snow month), Pluviôse (rain month), Ventôse (wind month), Germinal (germination month), Floréal (blossom month), Prairial (meadow month), Messidor (corn harvest month), Thermidor (heat month) and Fructidor (fruit month).* Children's names were even recommended to be derived from the names of the individual days. Author Jean-Alexandre Carney, created a system for naming children according to the Revolutionary calendar, suggesting that names are presented according to the gender of the child, day of birth and even time of birth. So a girl born at 9 in the morning would have a different name assigned than a girl born at 9 in the evening! This calendar did not last long though, with Napoleon bringing back the Gregorian calendar on the 1st January 1806, making the last day of the French Revolutionary calendar the 31st December 1805 or rather, Fléau, the 10th day of Nivôse of the year 14.

The 7-day week does not follow much logic as such nowadays, since it was first introduced to follow the lunar cycle of roughly 7 days, but with all the confusion that leap years introduced it is now not in sync. We probably stuck with the 7-day week to avoid more confusion and for religious reasons, but truth is, our current year and month system would still work just fine if we had 10 days per week like in the French Republican calendar or even 5 days per week for example. A 5-day week actually existed in Soviet Russia in 1929, when they decided to create these smaller work weeks, with days named after... colours; yellow, orange, red, purple and green! The calendars were even colour-coded to make life easier! Each citizen was given a different colour to represent their day off so as not to ever stop mass production. Due to the inevitable confusion,

89

the system was changed in 1932... to a 6-day week, but soon reverted to a 7-day week in 1940.

Our current names for the days of the week have a bit more of a story behind them than colours or numbers do, and many languages use planets and Gods to name the days. This was influenced by the Babylonians who named their days after the celestial bodies known to them at the time. In the English language for instance, Saturday, Sunday and Monday are named after Saturn, the Sun and the Moon respectively. In French, Mardi, Mercredi, Jeudi and Vendredi are named after Mars, Mercury, Jupiter and Venus. The remaining English week days, Tuesday, Wednesday, Thursday and Friday were interestingly named after Norse Gods due to German influence. The deities were, Tiw, Odin, Thor and Frigga, to form Tiw's day, Woden's day, Thor's day and Frige's day... close enough!

More recent attempts were proposed to try and figure out a better calendar system, some even wanting a calendar to have fixed days per year, meaning that every single date of a year would be assigned a specific day of the week and this would never change. I am pretty against this idea as this would remove the randomness that makes us human. British parliamentary member Mr. Ivor Thomas put it best when this was proposed in 1944 when he said: "I hope the Minister will not overlook one grave defect of this scheme, that every person would have the same day for his birthday every year. It is bad enough to be born on April 1st, but to have one's birthday always on a Monday would be perfectly intolerable. There is also the great historical objection. As this change has been suggested by a member of the traditional party may I as a member of the revolutionary party hope that we shall not destroy the precious links with Numa, Julius Caesar, and Gregory XIII which we have in our present calendar."

OK, so now humans can tell what day of the year it is, but how did they develop the system to organize the smaller time measurements? Measuring the time in one day is a completely different process from measuring years and months. The units of time need to be smaller, much smaller. Time is moving very fast in this realm and order must be reached somehow. The Egyptians are believed to be the first civilization on Earth to break up the day into smaller parts. Egyptian sundials as early as 1500 BC can be found to have divided the day (or the time between sunrise and sunset rather) into 12 approximately equal parts. Why it was divided into 12 parts and not say 10 is still debatable, but many experts believe that this is because of the counting system that the Egyptians got from the Sumerians. Rather than counting their fingers (10) they would count the individual joints on the fingers of one hand, excluding the thumb (12).

A sundial however needs one important thing to work, the Sun, and this is of course is not present after the sun sets. This meant that the day was divided into light and dark, day and night. The time of day could be measured, but night time could not. These ancient humans therefore needed to rely on things that could be seen at night, stars. Constellations were tracked in such a way that the night time was also divided into 12 parts, and once again, they were not completely equal parts. The idea of having the day divided into 24 parts was thus formed, 12 divisions of day and 12 divisions of night. All that was left was to make these divisions equal, and introduce what we humans now call the hour.

Around 135 BC, the Greek astronomer Hipparchus, is acknowledged as being the first person to divide the day into 24 equal parts. He built upon the Egyptian system and proposed to create 24 equal parts of the day based on the Equinox, which happens 2 days a year, once in March and once in September. On the Equinox, the periods of night and day are nearly exactly the same all over the world, 12 hours and 12 hours, due to the Sun shining directly on the equator. Once Hipparchus knew how long each equal part of day and night was, he could now divide it equally. Remember, there were no references to go by and he essentially created the length of the hour as we know today, but this hour needed to be divided too.

Using techniques that were passed on to the Babylonians by the Sumerians, Hipparchus set out to divide the hour into equal parts. When making astronomical calculations, the Babylonians used a sexagesimal system (60), probably due to how divisible the number was, as it was able to be divided by each of the first 6 numbers. Claudius Ptolemy built upon Hipparchus' work and further divided the 60 equal parts of the hour into another 60 parts each. In his essay Almagest, he called the first 60 equal parts as *partes minutae primae* or "first minutes" and the second 60 equal parts as *partes minutae secundae* or "second minutes". These divisions, as you probably have already guessed, became known as minutes and seconds as we know them today. Although it was not until mechanical clocks were created in the 14th century that these small units of time became commonly used. A second hand didn't even appear on a clock until 1680.

Technically though, the day didn't need to be divided this way at all and it could have easily been divided into 10 parts rather than 12 for example. During the French Revolution, in November 1793,

France did just that and replaced the 24 hour (12 and 12) system to decimal time with a 10-hour system, known as French Revolutionary time. The day was 10 hours long, each hour had 100 minutes and each minute had 100 seconds. This did not prove to be at all popular for some reason (maybe because everyone was so used to the previous system) and France went back to the original system in April 1795, just 17 months later. Decimal clocks and watches from this era can still be found today and are considered extremely rare and valuable.

Time-keeping nowadays is extremely accurate and most modern timepieces are only off by a few seconds. The atomic clock has an accuracy of less than one second every 6 million years! The second was defined as 1/86400 of the solar day until the year 1956. Technological advances after World War II made a more accurate definition necessary and it was redefined as 1/31,556,925.9747 of the tropical year. This was used until 1967 when scientists decided to redefine the second based on the electromagnetic wavelengths of the Atomic Clock. The 'second' is now defined as "the duration of 9192631770 cycles of the radiation corresponding to the transition between the two hyperfine levels of the ground state of the caesium 133 atom." Sounds about right...

This might sound odd, but could there be such a thing as time-keeping methods being too accurate? Apparently so. The reason being that the Earth's spin is decelerating very slowly due to tidal forces between the Moon and Earth and as a result the length of the solar day is reducing at a rate of 1.3 microseconds per day, which is around 1 second every 800 days. Now this is a problem because the time standard we use today, Coordinated Universal Time (UTC), uses both the Earth's rotation (astronomical time) and atomic clocks (atomic time) to help synchronize time. Since atomic clocks function at the same constant speed for millions of years, they are simply too accurate, unlike the Earth's rotation which is changing ever so slightly. To compensate for this, leap seconds are introduced into UTC, meaning that not all minutes have 60 seconds but a few rare minutes have 61 seconds, about 1 every 18 months.

Technological advances around the world were also responsible for creating what we call time-zones. Before travelling around the world and communicating long distance became a common occurrence, many cities had their own local times which were based on the times of sunset and sunrise. These would therefore be occurring at different times around the world but didn't become noticeable until technology made travelling long distance and telecommunications possible. Time zones were consequently needed for regions to keep the same time whilst allowing local time to be close to the real solar time.

Time-zones are based on imaginary lines called longitudinal lines that go from the North Pole to the South Pole and were originally created in the year 2 AD by Ptolemy whilst making a world atlas. Ptolemy placed the zero degree longitudinal line also known as the Prime Meridian through the west coast of Africa, but in the 18th century this was placed in various places, sometimes passing through London, Berlin and Paris. It was in the year 1880 that Greenwich in England became the constant Prime Meridian of the entire world. Since the Earth rotates at around 15 degrees per hour, it was decided that the Earth's 360 degrees would be divided by these 15 degrees to create 24 different zones. The time at the Prime Meridian (Greenwich) was known as Greenwich Mean Time (GMT) and time zones were created in 1883 that deducted or added on an hour depending on how many degrees west or east the area was from Greenwich.

The east coast of the United States for example had to follow Eastern Standard Time (EST) which was 75 degrees west of Greenwich and therefore 5 hours behind (GMT -5). Italy was on Central European Time (CET), 15 degrees east of Greenwich and therefore 1 hour had to be added (GMT +1). Although there should be just 24 different zones, various regions do not conform to the normal 1 hour increments, such as India which is UTC +5:30 and Nepal which is UTC +5:45, making many more than 24 time-zones. GMT and UTC are sometimes confused since they share the same time, however GMT is now (as of 1972) just a time-zone whereas UTC is a time-keeping standard. The common 21st century physiological phenomenon of jet-lag is in fact caused due to travelling through many time zones in a short period, and moving further east of the Prime Meridian causes more problems than travelling west as your body clock will need to be advanced!

Then just to confuse things a little bit more, we have Daylight Saving Time (DST), which came about in the early 20th century initially as a wartime measure for saving coal used to produce electrical power and to effectively make better use of natural light. The practice in essence lengthens evening daylight whilst giving up the usual sunrise times. Daylight Saving Time occurs when countries that apply this concept put their clocks forward by one hour at the start of spring only to put them back when autumn (Fall) is beginning (Spring forward, Fall back!). Neither GMT nor UTC change due to Daylight Savings, instead countries using DST change over to different time zones, for example Central European Time (CET) switches over to Central European Summer Time (CEST) and the UK switches to British Summer Time (BST). Ever since its inception there has been disagreement about whether its advantages are great enough to justify it. The main advantages include making better use of daylight, conserving energy that

95

would have been used to create artificial light instead, reduce traffic accidents by making sure roads are lit naturally in peak hours and extra commercial spending by both citizens and tourists. Previous concerns against the idea DST were due to farmers objecting that it would upset their routine, but this has ruled out with technological advances, although concerns still exist today with regard to health and in some countries the safety of persons leaving home in the morning when it's still dark is being questioned. Humans really did put a lot of time into creating the right time keeping systems!

However you measure it, your human life is still relatively short, so you should definitely make the most of it. Assuming you live a long and healthy life you would probably be looking at a total of around 30,000 days of living (approx. 80 years), which sounds like a lot but can pass extremely quickly, especially when you spend nearly 10,000 days (approx. 26 years) of it sleeping! Think about it like this, most humans sleep for 8 hours per night. If you are 30 years old and have 50 more years to live, reducing your sleeping time by just 1 hour a night can increase your time spent awake by 2 whole years, and there's a lot that can be done in 2 years! The average human spends around 10 years at work, if they are working 40-hour weeks starting at 20 years old and stopping at 65 years old. Time management in that respect could come in very handy, as there are many ways to get a good income without sacrificing 10 whole years of your life! Just to put things into perspective, you also spend nearly 2 years of life in a bathroom, 3 months of which are spent on a toilet!

As the saying goes, "When you are young, you have got a lot of time and all the energy to enjoy life, but no money. When you are in your middle years, you have got the money and all the energy, but no time. And when you are much older, you have got money and a lot of time, but no energy." The trick is to try and achieve all three at once!

Chapter 13: Unlucky For Some

Do you have Triskaidekaphobia? I hope you don't, because that would mean you would be very afraid of this chapter, particularly the number of this chapter. Yes, triskaidekaphobia is the fear of the number 13. This particular superstition however is quite a widespread one, entering into many aspects of our lives. Many airports do not have a 13th gate for example and many airplanes do not have a 13th aisle. The reason being, I guess, is that including this number would make superstitious people more anxious to fly and end up being unlucky in the long run for the airports and airlines themselves, with superstitious customers asking to change their flights and seating arrangements constantly. This superstition can also be seen in apartment buildings that lack a 13th floor and hotels or hospitals that do not have rooms numbered 13. Would the Apollo 13 mission have gone slightly better had it been given another number?

The origins of the fear of this odd number can be attributed to Scandinavian mythology, when 12 gods dining in Valhalla were unexpectedly joined by a 13th guest, Loki. The 12 gods tried to make Loki leave but as a result, the most liked god, Balder, was killed. Also, in Christianity at the Last Supper, Judas, the disciple who ultimately betrays Jesus, was seen as the 13th person to sit at table. As a result, many hosts have always avoided inviting 13 guests to sit at table, some fearing that if this does indeed happen, one of the guests will die before year end. I heard from a friend once that her superstitious grandmother who had invited 14 guests for a Christmas lunch, was very upset when one of them fell ill, and was left with the potentially unlucky prospect of 13 guests sitting at the table. To avoid this potentially deadly scenario, the host made her granddaughter invite a young neighbour to join the party, bringing the number up to 14 once again. This predicament would have been much easier to fix in France in the 1800s, were a professional 14th guest known as a quatorzième could be hired against payment!

However, before you start cancelling your dinner arrangements you might be consoled with the following story. In the 1880s, a club called The Thirteen Club was created to disprove the theory that the number 13 was unlucky and throughout its lifetime, five US presidents including Theodore Roosevelt were members. The Thirteen club used to meet on the 13th of the month and always had 13 guests seated at table. Members even passed under a ladder before being seated and also opened umbrellas indoors. According to records, none of the members died or had any bad luck whatsoever, some members even reported to have had good luck instead!

The date, Friday the 13th is seen as even unluckier than any regular 13th of the month and stems from the fact that Friday is not considered the best day throughout history, with the most notable examples being Eve giving Adam the dreaded apple on a Friday and Jesus being crucified on a Friday. There is also a term for being afraid of Friday the 13th, paraskevidekatriaphobia. No doubt, the horror film franchise, Friday the 13th, did little to ease concerns over this particular doubt.

As with so many things in this world however, different cultures have different superstitions. In countries that speak Spanish for example, it is Tuesday the 13th (martes trece) that is the unlucky date and not Friday, and it is known as Trezidavomartiofobia.

Tetraphobia, the fear of the number 4, is also common in various Asian countries due to the word for 4 in Mandarin being similar to the word for death. In Japan, the room number 43 is avoided in maternity wards, as it means "still birth". Funnily enough, in Italy, 13 is mostly considered a lucky number with 17 being the unlucky number instead. In fact, a direct-to-video parody horror movie "Shriek: If You Know What I Did Last Friday the Thirteenth" was released in Italy under the name "Shriek: Hai impegni per venerdì 17?" translated to "Shriek: Do You Have Something to Do on Friday the 17th?"). So I wouldn't be too worried about Friday the 13th, as you could always just take a trip to Italy and grab yourself some pizza when the dreaded date comes around!

The number 7 is usually a lucky number, associated with good, however if you break a mirror you supposedly get 7 years of bad luck. What's up with this? This superstition is actually quite an old one that originated before mirrors themselves existed. Before mirrors, all reflections of oneself were seen as magical, and similar to a portal were you could look into the future, a practice known as catoptromancy. Breaking such reflective device would therefore be akin to destroying your future, sometimes even losing one's soul, as it was believed that mirrors did not just reflect ones physical persona but even the spiritual. The Romans who first invented the mirror, seem to have also developed the 7 year bad luck superstition, as they believed that one's life would restart every 7 years and therefore you would have to wait for this cycle to pass. Another theory regarding this superstition is that mirrors were very expensive in the 15th century, so owners used to tell their servants this myth in order for them to be extra careful. If only we could use this trick for other things nowadays, like taking the last slice of pizza!

The walking under a ladder and opening an umbrella indoors superstitions seem to be quite practical to be honest, it's probably not a good idea anyway, you know, especially when there's someone balancing on top of a ladder or when it's not raining inside. One reason why walking under a ladder is seen to be unlucky is that hangmen used ladders to hang people from the gallows and therefore walking under a ladder would be tempting fate so to speak. Other theories include the fact that a ladder leaning against a wall, or a free standing ladder, would form triangles which could signify the Holy Trinity (Father, Son and the Holy Spirit), so walking under it would be breaking this trinity, and therefore blasphemous. A ladder also rested against the crucifix when Jesus was crucified, which further adds to this superstition.

There is speculation to the origins of the opening of umbrellas indoors superstition, with some even going back to the Ancient Egyptians. Ancient Egyptians? I didn't even think umbrellas went back that far! But yes, we are talking about sun umbrellas or parasols here, the type that were used to keep royalty sheltered from the heat of the sun. Opening this sun umbrella indoors would apparently have offended the Sun god and so would have been avoided at all costs. The modern rain umbrella superstition hardly seems related to sun umbrellas though, and this seems to have originated in England in the 18th century. Back then, rain umbrellas were big and bulky objects, so opening them inside a house in a confined space was a dangerous feat in itself, therefore the superstition most likely came about to stop people, especially children, from playing with them indoors.

Last but definitely not least, we cannot forget the dark feline, the ebony kitty… the black cat. If we had to take a look at ancient Egyptian times (which seems to happen quite a lot), we would find that cats, of any colour or description were worshipped and not ever feared in any way. The Goddess Bast was in fact a black cat! This seemed to change during medieval times, when black cats were seen as witches' helpers or even witches themselves, and therefore not worshipped anymore. A black cat was viewed as being the devil himself! Could it be that cuddly Professor Wiggles is really the spawn of Satan?

In England this was never the case and black cats were seen to be a positive thing if anything, however many other parts of Europe did not share the same views. A black cat crossing your path would mean that the devil himself was watching you, prohibiting your eventual entrance to heaven. Unfortunately this superstition was the cause of a lot of grief for black cats back in the day, including their owners, thinking that they were witches, and by grief I mean death. Western culture has come to believe this negative stereotyping more and more, backed up by the entertainment industry, and a good example of a time to see this is Halloween. Many black cats are adopted during this period for the sole purpose of being a costume prop or some sort of decoration (similar to rabbits during Easter). To avoid the potential abandonment of our furry friends, animal shelters often restrict adoption of black cats till after Halloween passes. Statistically, a black cat is the least adopted colour of cat. You would probably be safe in Japan if you were a black cat, as they are usually good luck, however like many other things, this is slowly changing with the ever-present influence of the West!

Chapter 14: Would You Rather?

This is a great game for a group of humans to play, and can provide hours of entertainment. It really gets conversations flowing and you can learn a lot of new things about people whom you thought you knew everything about. The rules of the game itself are very simple, but the questions posed can lead to dilemmas that are anything but easy. The game is played by asking what another person would rather do out of a choice of two options. There is no right or wrong answer and you just need to choose one. You cannot choose both of the options or neither of them. An answer must be given. Below are some of the harder and more interesting questions which have been compiled for you. Some are choices having two positive options, while others are slightly harder as they have two negative outcomes:

Would you rather have a guaranteed $100,000 OR a 50-50 chance at $1,000,000?

Would you rather be the smartest person OR the most popular person you know?

Would you rather be blind OR deaf?

Would you rather be stabbed to death OR buried alive?

Would you rather be super-fast OR super-strong?

Would you rather look strong and actually be weak OR look weak and actually be strong?

Would you rather be poor and work at a job you love OR be wealthy and work at a job you hate?

Would you rather be blind OR not be able to talk for the rest of your life?

Would you rather be able to become invisible OR be able to fly as a super power?

Would you rather have one wish granted now OR three wishes granted over 10 years?

Would you rather see into the future OR be able to change the past?

Would you rather spend five years in prison and become wealthy OR never go to jail but never be rich?

Would you rather walk naked in a snow storm OR wear a boiler suit in the desert?

Would you rather spend five years in prison for something you didn't do OR ten years for something you did do?

Would you rather have hiccups forever OR always feel like you need to sneeze but never be able to?

Would you rather make love to a donkey and no one would know OR, NOT make love to a donkey, but everyone would think that you did? (Replace 'a donkey' at will!)

Would you rather know how you're going to die OR know when you're going to die?

Would you rather live ten 100 year lives OR one 1000 year life?

Would you rather have the best house in a bad neighbourhood OR the worst house in a nice neighbourhood?

Would you rather be gossiped about all the time OR never talked about?

Would you rather be rich and unattractive OR poor and very attractive?

Would you rather be stranded on a desert island alone OR with somebody you hate?

Would you rather find true love OR 10 million dollars?

Would you rather forget who you were OR forget who everyone else was?

Would you rather never watch TV again OR never use the internet again?

Would you rather not be able to use the telephone OR e-mail?

Would you rather only be able to whisper OR only be able to shout?

Would you rather be able to fly OR stop time?

Would you rather have a missing finger OR an extra toe?

Would you rather go through life unable to ask any questions OR unable to answer any questions?

Would you rather save the life of someone that you're very close to OR save the lives of 20 strangers?

Would you rather be the first to die from your group of friends OR the last?

Would you rather have to stand all day OR sit all day?

Would you rather be able to control the weather OR walk through walls?

Would you rather have superhuman intelligence OR superhuman strength?

Would you rather go back in time and meet your ancestors OR go into the future and meet your great-great grandchildren?

Would you rather have more time OR more money?

Would you rather have a pause button OR a rewind button on your life?

Would you rather physically OR mentally never age?

Would you rather know the moment of your own death OR the moment of the death of the person closest to you?

Would you rather be the worst player on the best team OR the best player on a mediocre team?

Chapter 15: Of A

'A'. The first letter of our alphabet, and a good place to start some might say! The letter 'A' finds its origins in an unlikely animal, the ox. Proto-Sinaitic script developing from Egyptian hieroglyphs of an ox head, created the foundations of the 'A' shape that we know today. If you turn an 'A' upside down you may notice that it resembles the head of an ox complete with horns. The Phoenician *aleph* (derived from the Semitic word *alef*, meaning ox), which was essentially the ox head turned on its side, and the first letter of their alphabet, was the earliest form of the modern 'A'. The ox was the head of beasts at that time so presumably this is why it was also the first letter of their alphabet. It was not a vowel in the Phoenician alphabet as their alphabet contained no vowels, but instead represented a breathing sound, a consonant known as a glottal stop. An example of a glottal stop in modern English is the dash in the phrase "uh-oh!" It was the Greeks who first started using this letter as the vowel we know today, eventually turning it right side up, or rather, the way we currently write it.

The letter 'A' can take different forms. These are known as allographs, which is when the same letter has alternatives, such as when upper-case and lower-case letters are different from each other and when there are stylistic variations of these. The upper-case 'A' and the lower case 'a' are evidently very different from each other, but the lower-case letter also has different ways that it can be shaped. There is the 'a' known as the 'double-storey a', which has a top hook, and the 'ɑ' known as the 'single-storey ɑ', which has no top hook. It is purely a stylistic difference, one simply became popular through printing while the other became popular through handwriting. Statistically, the letter 'A' is the third most used letter of our alphabet, with the letter 'E' taking first place and 'T' coming in a close second.

10 short ramblings beginning with the letter 'A':

1. Aardvark: The first or second word in the English dictionary (depending on whether you consider the word 'a') due to its spelling, with a 'double-a' at the beginning. The word is borrowed from an Afrikaans (language descended from Dutch, spoken mainly in Africa) word, which describes this nocturnal mammal, meaning 'earth pig'. Their closest relative is not the pig at all though but the elephant.

2. Andy and Bill's law: This originally started off as a running joke at computer conferences in the 1990s, stating that "What Andy giveth, Bill taketh away." This was referring to Andy Grove, who was CEO of Intel back then and Bill Gates, who was the CEO of Microsoft. The law meant that when Intel release a computer chip to the market which had higher capabilities, Microsoft would release updated software that would use up all of the new chips power.

3. Amara's law: Roy Amara, past president of The Institute for the Future is best known for his statement (paraphrased by Robert X. Cringely) which became known as Amara's law: "We tend to overestimate the effect of a technology in the short run and underestimate the effect in the long run."

4. Asimov's three laws of robotics: These three rules were written by science fiction author Isaac Asimov in 1942: "A robot may not injure a human being or, through inaction, allow a human being to come to harm. A robot must obey orders given it by human beings except where such orders would conflict with the First Law. A robot must protect its own existence as long as such protection does not conflict with the First or Second Law."

5. Allen's rule: This eco-geographical rule states that the body shapes and the proportions of endotherms (previously known as warm-blooded animals) differ due to climatic temperature by either decreasing the exposed surface area to minimize heat loss in cold climates or increasing the exposed surface area to maximize heat loss in hot climates. Therefore body parts such as limbs and ears are shorter and more compact in animals living in cold climates and can be seen in humans too. This rule is named after Joel Asaph Allen who described it in 1877.

6. Aurora Borealis: The Northern Lights as they are known, or the Southern Lights (Aurora Australis) are spectacular displays of light that can be seen in the sky from particular areas. The display of light is formed when electrically charged particles from outer space enter into the Earth's magnetosphere, accelerate along the Earth's magnetic field which is concentrated at the poles, and then collide with gases in the upper atmosphere. This produces excess energy as a by-product which is released in the form of the auroras. Yellow and green displays are formed when the charged particles collide with oxygen and violet, blue and red display when they collide with nitrogen. The Northern lights are best seen in winter time in areas far north such as Greenland, Iceland, Norway, Sweden, Finland, Alaska, Canada and Russia. The Southern lights are best seen from Australia, New Zealand, The Falkland Islands, Argentina and the island of South Georgia. Seeing these lights is definitely on my bucket list!

7. Abilene paradox: The Abiline paradox involves a group taking a decision that is not favoured by most members or even all members of the group. Each member of the group would be simply going with the flow thinking that they are pleasing the other members and vice versa. The term was coined by Jerry B. Harvey, author of "The Abilene Paradox and Other Meditations on Management." He explains the paradox using a story of a family trip that nobody wanted to go on:

"On a hot afternoon visiting in Coleman, Texas, the family is comfortably playing dominoes on a porch, until the father-in-law suggests that they take a trip to Abilene (53 miles north) for dinner. The wife says, 'Sounds like a great idea.' The husband, despite having reservations because the drive is long and hot, thinks that his preferences must be out-of-step with the group and says, 'Sounds good to me. I just hope your mother wants to go.' The mother-in-law then says, 'Of course I want to go. I haven't been to Abilene in a long time.' The drive is hot, dusty, and long. When they arrive at the cafeteria, the food is as bad as the drive. They arrive back home four hours later, exhausted. One of them dishonestly says, 'It was a great trip, wasn't it?' The mother-in-law says that, actually, she would rather have stayed home, but went along since the other three were so enthusiastic. The husband says, 'I wasn't

delighted to be doing what we were doing. I only went to satisfy the rest of you.' The wife says, 'I just went along to keep you happy. I would have had to be crazy to want to go out in the heat like that.' The father-in-law then says that he only suggested it because he thought the others might be bored. The group sits back, perplexed that they together decided to take a trip which none of them wanted. They each would have preferred to sit comfortably, but did not admit to it when they still had time to enjoy the afternoon."

The way to combat this problem is to create a comfortable environment that makes room for disagreement and lets all members of a group have a voice.

8. Avocado: Planting an avocado tree is fun and quite simple! After you have finished taking a picture of your avocado toast for Instagram, do not throw away the remains of the avocado! Wash the seed and pierce it gently with 4 toothpicks to allow it to rest over a glass filled with water, with the broad end slightly submerged in the water. The glass should be kept in a warm place out of direct sunlight and the water should be topped up when necessary. Roots will start to sprout out of the bottom of the seed and a stem at the top after around 4-6 weeks (and it's amazing to see!). When the stem reaches around 6 inches trim it halfway to 3 inches, and when the roots became thick it is ready to be planted. The seed should be left half-exposed and watered frequently, with the soil being slightly moist but not too wet. When the stem is 12 inches high trim it halfway again to 6 inches. When the tree starts to outgrow the pot, you would need to replant it and this is best done in the springtime. If you are expecting fruit to grow immediately then this might be the wrong tree for you, as it could take as long as 4 to 13 years to happen!

9. Asch conformity experiments: In 1951, at Swarthmore College, psychologist Solomon Asch conducted a series of experiments with the aim of studying conformity. In these experiments Asch recruited volunteers on the pretence of participating in a visual test, with the aim of matching various line lengths to one another. The volunteers were singled out and introduced to a group of other volunteers, who were really actors. The group was then shown a line and asked to match it to the correct size line from a selection of lines of different lengths. The answers were read out loud one by one by the actors until it was the real volunteer's turn. At the beginning the actors would choose the correct answer, but after a while they all began to give the wrong answer, even though the correct answer was obvious to see. The result was that quite a percentage of volunteers conformed to the wrong answer (36.8%), with 75% of the volunteers giving at least one wrong answer.

10. The only two countries whose name begins with an 'A' but doesn't end in an 'A' are Afghanistan and Azerbaijan.

Here is a list of countries beginning with 'A' and their capital cities, followed by their flags:

Afghanistan: Kabul

Albania: Tirana

Algeria: Algiers

Andorra: Andorra la Vella

Angola: Luanda

Antigua and Barbuda: Saint John's

Argentina: Buenos Aires

Armenia: Yerevan

Australia: Canberra

Austria: Vienna

Azerbaijan: Baku

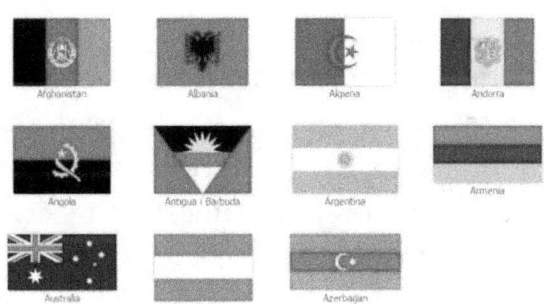

Chapter 16: The Upper Hand

The playing of games is an integral part of human culture and every single human, no matter how serious they decide to become in their later years of life, has played a game at one time or another. Evidence of physical games have been found that are thousands of years old, with Mancala boards from the 6th century AD found in Ethiopia, Royal Game of Ur boards from Iraq dating to 2600 BC and Senet boards found in Egypt that go as far back as the year 3500 BC!

As 21st century humans though, we are spoilt for choice and now we have literally thousands upon thousands of games available to us, be they physical games or the more recent addition of video games. It is no secret that humans are competitive animals, it is part of how we evolved, and how we live our day to day lives. Some people just learn to deal with it better than others. You would probably be lying if you said you do not feel better when you win, even the simplest of games. There is a sense of pride in every win, no matter how small. Some games have been played by many of us for years, maybe losing at them more often than winning, most probably due to the fact that we have never properly stopped to examine the game long enough, and ask ourselves why. Even though we might have played them countless times, certain games do indeed have tricks, and knowing them, like everything in life, will give you the competitive edge over your opponent.

Noughts and crosses, Xs and Os, tic-tac-toe, OXO. Whatever name you know this game by, you have probably played it as a child, but it still can be used by adults to solve disputes. It is the two player game where you draw a 3 x 3 grid (like a hashtag #) on a paper and take turns drawing Xs and Os, trying to get 3 of the same in a row, vertically, horizontally or diagonally. This basic game can actually be mastered very easily, and knowing some key points will allow you to never lose the game. The good news is that if you play tic-tac-toe correctly you can never lose. The bad news is that if your opponent plays correctly then you can never win. You will always end up with a tie if you both play perfectly. This is different to the popular game Connect 4, where the first player will always end up with a win, if both play perfectly, and the first player places his first piece in the middle column (4th column out of 7). Both these games have been solved, the general rule being that since there is no randomness as such, and there are a finite number of moves then the game can be technically solved. Computer programs have been created to play both these games perfectly and have sometimes been credited with having AI (artificial intelligence). This is not quite so because the game has been solved and the computer is simply following a script and not reasoning in any way as it would with unsolved games. Here are some tricks to never lose at tic-tac-toe:

First of all for the purposes of this guide, X will always start first and O will play second. There are 3 positions that one can play, the center, a side or a corner.

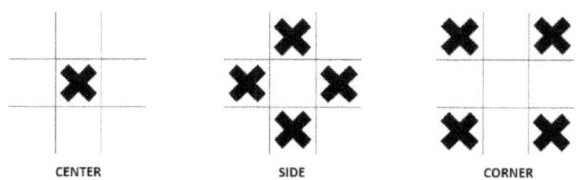

CENTER   SIDE   CORNER

If you are starting you have a greater advantage of winning. Make sure you place the first X in any corner. If you rotate the grid you will notice it makes no difference. If your opponent does NOT mark the center then you will win, just by marking any other corner. Your opponent will then block you (if not, then you would win there and then). The next thing for you to do is to mark the next open corner and you have now successfully trapped your opponent and have two options to win. After your opponent blocks one of your options you can now win the game.

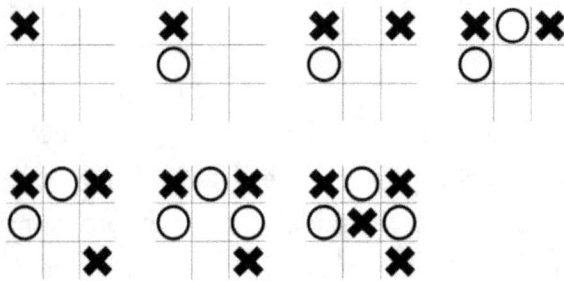

If your opponent places an O in the center after you play a corner then it is a little harder to win. You first must go to the opposite corner of where you started. If the opponent chooses any other corner then you will just need to play in the final corner (to block their move) and form a trap, by once again having two options to win. After the second player blocks one of your options you can now win the game.

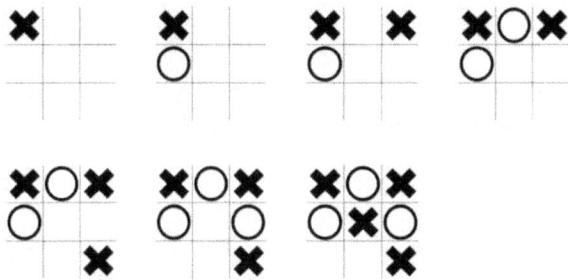

Not to make the game too repetitive you can also start play in the center. If your opponent places his O in an edge square then you have already won the game. Simply mark a corner in your second move and the opponent will have no choice but to block you. You will then just need to block his attempt and you would have trapped him, having two options to win. After your opponent blocks one of your options you can now win the game.

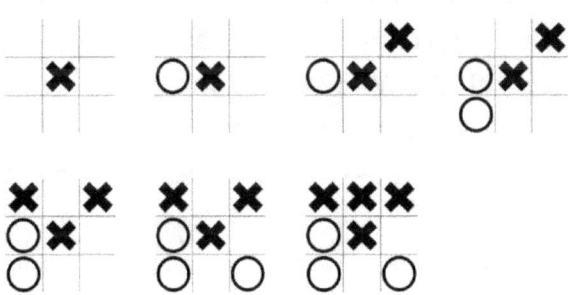

If after starting play in the center, the opponent places his O in a corner then it is slighter harder to win. You would need to place your X in the opposite corner and hope your opponent's next move is in a side square as the game would otherwise end in a tie with perfect play.

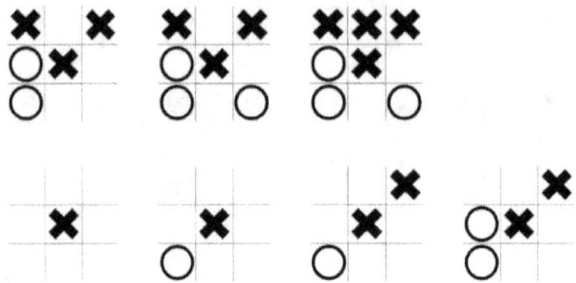

When playing first always avoid playing a side square as your first move. If you are playing second, use the information I previously gave to force a tie (or hope your opponent is simply a weak one, never read about these tricks or does not play perfectly!)

Rock-paper-scissors (RPS), *roshambo* (or earwig-human-elephant in Indonesia!) is another one of those childhood games that everyone played and knows about, and is still used by older humans when a decision needs to be taken quickly. Originating in Asia and moving to the Western world as late as the 20th century, it is seemingly a game of no skill and luck. That might not be completely true however, especially when you find out that there is a World Rock Paper Scissors Society (which originally started off as a joke) that holds world championships of the game, and many of the same competitors finish in top positions. Could this simply be a coincidence?

If you have been living under a rock (paper!) all your life, then you would need me to explain to you that RPS is one of the world's most common decision-making solutions, right up there with tossing a coin. There are a total of 3 moves which would all have 3 different outcomes against an opponent's move. Rock beats scissors, loses to paper and ties against itself. Paper beats rock, loses to scissors and ties against itself. Scissors beats paper, loses to rock and ties against itself. Taking the game at face value, we would see that mathematically it would seem to make sense to play randomly, making sure that each move is played exactly one third of the time. This is called a Nash Equilibrium strategy, named after John Forbes Nash Jr, of A Beautiful Mind fame. In a nutshell, both players are in Nash equilibrium if they are both making the best decisions they can, taking into account each other's decision, while both of their decisions remain unchanged. This would mean that the players' moves have to be totally random, with each move unaffected by any outside influence, such as the opponent's previous move.

A group of Chinese researchers led by Zhijian Wang, at Zhejiang University in China put the above theory to the test and got some interesting results. It was true that overall, in the long run, each move will have been chosen approximately one third of the time, however some curious patterns emerged that maybe should have been obvious from the start. Humans, being humans, can never be expected to play completely at random and certain psychology and reactions must come into play. They found out that winners were repeating their winning moves while losers were moving on to the next one. The researchers called them conditional social responses, and they believe that these might be ingrained in the way we think. It indeed might seem expected that if a player is doing well with one move he will stick with it, while a player continuously losing with one move will change it to the move that beats the move they lost to. So if you win again with rock, it is more than likely that the opponent's move will be the move that beat rock, which is paper, and therefore you should anticipate your next move to be scissors.

- If you won the last round with rock (opponent had scissors) then scissors should be your next move.

- If you won the last round with scissors (opponent had paper) then paper should be your next move.

- If you won the last round with paper (opponent had rock) then rock should be your next move.

If you are in a losing position (assuming your opponent does not know all this game theory), don't panic. You should take it for granted that your opponent will repeat the last winning move again, so your next move should simply be the one that beats it.

- If you lost the last round with rock (opponent had paper) then scissors should be your next move.

- If you lost the last round with scissors (opponent had rock) then paper should be your next move.

- If you lost the last round with paper (opponent had scissors) then rock should be your next move.

Of course there is a limit to an opponent using the same move, as that would seemingly feel predictable for most players. So after two successive moves that are the same by the opponent, play the hand that would have lost to their two moves as they are unlikely to repeat their move a third time.

- If your opponent plays rock two times in a row, then scissors should be your next move.

- If your opponent plays scissors two times in a row, then paper should be your next move.

- If your opponent plays paper two times in a row, then scissors should be your next move.

All of the above information will only come into play after the first crucial throw, which is seemingly just a lucky guess. We have to rely on other information to try and gain the competitive edge over here, such as the fact that rock is played more often as the first move by males (perhaps due to its masculine connotations). Also, statistics have found that rock is the most commonly used with 35.4% of moves, paper very close at 35% and scissors at 29.6%. Considering these facts, if you only play one round, and not a best out of 3 for example, it might be wise to choose paper as your only move, given that men would choose rock and that scissors is the least chosen of the three. You are now armed with extra knowledge that will allow you to win the next drink at the bar!

You might find that this game could get you more than just a drink though, as in 2005 it decided the fate of which auction house should sell $20 million worth of impressionist paintings. Takashi Hashiyama, president of a Japanese electronics firm was impressed by both Christie's and Sotheby's presentations and therefore told them that the winner of a rock-paper-scissors game would get the contract. Sotheby's viewed this as a game of chance and did not choose a move with any particular strategy in mind. Christie's on the other hand, did extensive research, including speaking with the director's young twin daughters who gave the following advice: "Everybody knows you always start with scissors." and "Rock is way too obvious... since they were beginners, scissors was definitely the safest." Adding that if the other side would also choose scissors and another round was required, the correct play would be to stick to scissors because, "Everybody expects you to choose rock." One round was all that was needed however, since Christie's produced scissors and Sotheby's hand was paper, meaning that Christie's got the contract to sell $20 million worth of art and received nearly $2 million in commission as a result!

"I like rock-paper-scissors... two-thirds. Rock breaks scissors: these scissors are bent, they're destroyed, I can't cut stuff... I lose! Scissors cuts paper: this is strips, this is not even paper, this can take me forever to put back together... you got me! Paper covers rock: rock is fine, no structural damage to rock. Rock can break through paper at any point, just say the word. Paper sucks. It should be... rock, dynamite with a cuttable wick, scissors."

– Demetri Martin

Chapter 17: No Offence

It is a well-known stereotype that blondes are supposedly more promiscuous and less intelligent than humans of another hair colour. It would seem like it would be obvious that this is not actually the case, but a team of scientists from Stanford University went through all the trouble of challenging this stereotype for us. Apparently a single letter change in our genetic code, chromosome 12 to be precise, is responsible for the difference in hair colour. The scientists emphasized that this switch affects only the hair follicle cells and other cells including the brain cells would definitely not be affected. Therefore disproving this stereotype once and for all. Thank you science, but this is probably one thing we didn't really need you to prove for us!

This label however, must have come about from somewhere. In 1925, in Anita Loos' novel 'Gentlemen Prefer Blondes', we find the fictional character Lorelei Lee fitting this description perfectly. This character was seen as shallow and superficial, simply using her good looks to get her way and move forward in life. Marilyn Monroe catapulted this typecast to greater heights when she played Lorelei in the 1953 movie 'Gentleman Prefer Blondes' and again when she was cast in a very similar role as Pola Debevoise in 'How to Marry a Millionaire'.

Feminism has reduced the impact of the negative stereotype tremendously but we still notice the effects of this nowadays. In 1999, a study conducted asking both men and women to rate the intelligence of a subject with different coloured wigs all rated the blonde as less intelligent. Another study this time in 2004, had blondes complete certain tests before and after reading blonde jokes and in fact after reading the jokes they performed considerably slower and worse. This effect is known as the stereotype threat, where a group, in this case blondes, would be affected by the pre-existing negative stereotype that they are being reminded about and feel afraid that they will indeed confirm this theory.

Sociologist Christie Davies in fact found that many jokes involving unintelligent people that exist nowadays have the same themes and punchlines as other negative-stereotype jokes in many different countries. The blonde jokes first started their life as sorority-girl jokes in the 1980s in the USA and then appeared as dumb-blonde jokes in Holland in the 1990s. Jokes about Belgians were then converted into these dumb-blonde jokes and in the UK the dumb-blonde has been converted into Essex girl jokes to give a more local feel. The truth is that these type of jokes could always be said in a more general way, such as, "stupid man" or "unintelligent woman" rather than being very specific, yet for some reason this specificness (is that a word?) makes them funnier than they would otherwise be.

I believe that at the end of the day, jokes are simply jokes and nobody should ever get offended by them as by doing so you are in essence implying that there is an element of truth in that joke. Dolly Parton once said: "I'm not offended by all the dumb-blonde jokes because I know I'm not dumb... and I also know that I'm not blonde." One should feel confident enough not to feel offended when a joke is being told that hits one of their characteristics, be it their gender, nationality, religion, race or even hair colour! Being offended should not be a 21st century thing for a human to do anymore. Stephen Fry put it best in my opinion, when he once said:

"It's now very common to hear people say, 'I'm rather offended by that.' As if that gives them certain rights. It's actually nothing more... than a whine. 'I find that offensive.' It has no meaning, it has no purpose, it has no reason to be respected as a phrase. 'I am offended by that.' Well, so f***ing what."

With that being said, here are some of those famous blonde jokes that we have been talking about, some deal with the characteristics of low IQ and others of promiscuity, so feel free to replace "blonde" with another word should you choose to feel 'offended', but remember there is really no truth in them anyway, so one should not need to feel offended in the first place!

A blonde walks into a library and asks the librarian, "Can I have a hamburger and fries please?" The librarian replies, "Sorry, this is a library." The blonde WHISPERS, "Oh, I'm sorry. May I have a hamburger and fries please?"

A blonde, a brunette, and a redhead all die and in order to get into heaven, they must walk up 100 steps, each step containing a joke. The trick is that they must not laugh. The brunette goes first and laughs at the first step and is sent to hell. The redhead goes next and makes it to the tenth step before she laughs. Finally, it is the blondes turn. She gets all the way up to the 99th step before she laughs. God asks her, "You were so close! Why did you laugh?" to which she responds, "I just got the first joke!"

A blonde was driving her kids to Disney Land. When they were about half way there, the blonde saw a sign that said "Disney Land, Left" so the blonde turned back around and went home.

There was this guy who was married to a blonde, and each night he came home with a new blonde joke. One night the wife got mad and decided to show him that she wasn't dumb. She spent the whole next day learning all her countries and capitals. That night when he got home he told his joke. She says, "I'm not so dumb. I know all of the countries and capitals. Go ahead, quiz me." He thought for a moment and asked, "What is the capital of England?" She quickly replied, "E"!

A highway patrolman pulled alongside a speeding car on the freeway. Glancing at the car, he was astounded to see that the blonde behind the wheel was knitting! Realizing that she wasn't noticing his flashing lights and siren, the trooper put down his window, turned on his bullhorn and yelled, "PULL OVER!" "NO!" the blonde yelled back, "IT'S A SCARF!"

A blonde asked someone what time it was, and they told her it was half past eight. The blonde, with a puzzled look on her face replied, "You know, it's the strangest thing, I have been asking that question all day, and each time I get a different answer."

A married couple were awakened by a call at two o'clock in the morning. The wife, a blonde, picked up the phone, listened a moment and said, "How should I know, that's 200 miles from here!" and hung up. Her husband asked, "Who was that?" She replied, "I don't know. Some woman wanting to know if the coast is clear."

A young blonde woman is very upset because she fears her husband is having an affair, so she goes to a gun shop and buys a revolver. One day she comes home and finds her husband in bed with a beautiful redhead. She grabs the gun and holds it to her own head. The husband jumps out of bed, begging and pleading with

126

her not to shoot herself. Hysterically the blonde responds to the husband, "Shut up... you're next!"

A blonde has sharp pains in her side, so she goes to the hospital. The doctor examines her and says, "You have acute appendicitis." The blonde says, "That's sweet, doc, but I came here to get medical help."

A blonde ordered a pizza and was asked if she wanted it cut in six or twelve pieces.

"Six, please. I could never eat twelve pieces."

A worker went into the office kitchen one morning and found a new blonde girl painting the walls. She was wearing a new fur coat and a nice denim jacket. Thinking this was a little strange, he asked her why she was wearing them rather than old clothes or an overall. She showed him the instructions on the paint can, "For best results, put on two coats".

A brunette is trying to get across a river and suddenly she spots a blonde on the other side. She yells over to the blonde "Hey, excuse me! How do I get over to the other side?" And after a quick survey of the river, the blonde calls back "You ARE on the other side!"

There once was a magic mirror which killed anyone who lied to it. One day a brunette was doing her makeup and said to herself, "I think I'm the smartest woman ever!" She immediately dropped dead. The next day a redhead was doing her hair and said to herself, "I think I'm the prettiest woman alive!" She immediately dropped dead. Finally, the following day, a blonde was flossing her teeth. She stopped and said to herself "I think..." and dropped dead.

A blonde, a brunette and a redhead are stuck on an island. One day, the three of them are walking along the beach and discover a magic lamp. They rub it, and sure enough, out pops a genie. The genie says, "Since I can only grant three wishes, you may each have one." The brunette says, "I've been stuck here for years. I miss my family, my husband, and my life. I just want to go home." POOF! The brunette gets her wish and she is returned to her family. Then, the red head says, "I've been stuck here for years as well. I miss my family, my husband, and my life. I wish I could go home too." POOF! The redhead gets her wish and she is returned to her family. The blonde starts crying uncontrollably. The genie asks, "My dear, what's the matter?" The blonde whimpers, "I wish my friends were still here."

A blonde walks into a doctor's office and says: "Doctor, what's the problem with me? When I touch my arm, it hurts... When I touch my leg, ouch, it hurts... When I touch my head, it hurts... When I touch my chest, ouch, it really hurts!" The doctor replies: "Your finger is broken."

A blonde rings up an airline. She asks, "How long are your flights from the US to England?" The woman on the other end of the phone says, "Just a minute." The blonde says, "Thanks!" and hangs up.

Q. Why did the blonde stare at a carton of orange juice for 3 hours?

A. Because it said concentrate.

Q. Why did the blonde get fired from the M&Ms factory?

A. For throwing out the W's.

Q. Why did the blonde get so excited after she finished her jigsaw puzzle in only 6 months?

A. Because on the box it said, "from 2-4 years."

Q. What is the definition of gross ignorance?

A. 144 blondes.

Q. What do you call a blonde with 2 brain cells?

A. Pregnant

Q. What do you call it when a blonde dies her hair brunette?

A. Artificial intelligence.

Q. What do you call a blonde skeleton in the closet?

A. Last year's hide and seek champion.

Q. What did the blonde's right leg say to the left leg?

A. Nothing. They've never met.

Q. Why did the blonde like the car with a sunroof?

A. More leg-room!

Q. How does a blonde turn on the light after making love?

A. Opens the car door.

Q. How does a blonde have safe sex?

A. Locks the car doors.

Chapter 18: How Much Is That Doggie In The Window? One Million Dollars!

Wouldn't it be great if the government decided to print lots of extra money and send everybody one million dollars? No it wouldn't. But wouldn't you be able to buy a great big house and that sports car you always wanted? No you wouldn't. The reason why you would not be able to do this is inflation. Inflation, simply put, is an increase in prices and a decrease in the value of the money used to buy these products. Printing lots of money would simply increase the amount of currency and as a result the demand for products, but not the amount of actual products. This is where 'supply and demand' comes into play.

If the demand for a product increases but the amount of products remain the same then you would have a shortage of products so prices would increase. Conversely, if the demand for a product decreases and the supply remains the same, there would be a surplus of products so prices would decrease. This is known as an indirect relationship, where if one variable increases the other decreases. In the case of printing more money, you would still have the same amount of products but a bigger demand now, so even though you have more money, your money would be worth less.

If 10 humans each have 1 dollar and there are just 10 oranges worth one dollar each, then everybody is happy and they can buy one orange each. If the government prints more money and now doubles everyone's dollar to 2 dollars, the 10 people would not be able to buy 2 oranges each as there are still just 10 oranges. The price of the oranges would need to inflate to 2 dollars per orange to make up for this. So even though you have more money it is now worth less than before, as previously 1 dollar bought 1 orange and now 2 dollars buys 1 orange. Therefore, if you doubled everyone's money, prices would also need to be doubled!

It is normal for inflation to occur gradually in every country over a number of years. For example, the Ford Model T, one of the first mass-produced cars, was priced at the $600 mark in the USA in 1914, applying an increase of 2265% inflation would bring the price to around $14,000, quite close to starting prices of small cars nowadays. However, whilst this inflation happened naturally, it is when inflation rises very rapidly in a short period of time that a country should worry. This is known as hyper-inflation and can be caused, among other things, by printing extra money.

There are many examples of hyper-inflation taking place around the globe. One of the most famous examples is 1920s Germany (or the Weimar Republic as it was called from 1919 to 1933) which faced such great hyper-inflation that left its currency practically worthless. This was brought about due to compensation payments that Germany was finding increasingly difficult to pay post World War I, and they printed more money as a consequence. As a result of this, prices soared, with everyday items such as bread now sporting exorbitant price tags. A loaf of bread that used to cost 1 mark in 1919 rose to 250 marks in January 1923 and by November 1923, when hyper-inflation was at its peak, was a tremendous 200,000,000,000 marks. That's 200 billion marks!

The saying "not worth the paper it's written on" took on a whole new meaning, with people writing notes on actual paper money as it was cheaper to do so than buying a notepad. At one point hyper-inflation was so bad that prices doubled every 4 days. There are stories of restaurant patrons sitting down for a meal which would increase in price as they dined! Due to this, prices were not written on menus anymore and it was not uncommon for customers to negotiate the price of a meal with the restaurant prior to making their order to prevent any price hikes. Money was used as wallpaper and children used it to make paper kites, while stacks of currency replaced toy bricks. Workers were paid in large amounts of money every day at specific times and would rush out to buy household goods so as not to lose the value of the cash given. These workers would fill up suitcases with money every single day and once there was even a situation where a suitcase full of money was stolen just for the suitcase itself, with the money being left behind!

Yugoslavia went through a similarly rough time in 1993. Using up all of its currency reserves, Yugoslavia resorted to printing money, resulting in severe inflation. Despite printing money though, it still did not have currency to keep the country running and it soon started to crumble. Government fuel stations were closed down and citizens had to use public transport rather than their own cars, but the government did not have enough fuel to run all buses and had to work with less than half. Buses were crowded as a result of this and ticket money could not even be collected due to the situation, making the government lose more money in the process. The government did not have enough resources to turn on the heating in government apartments, so the residents used electrical heaters, overloading the system and forcing the electric company to enforce blackouts to save energy. Inflation levels were increasing at a rapid rate every single day and one interesting story highlights this. Government telephone bills used to be collected by the postal workers and customers put off paying these bills until the inflation was so high that the bill's value was reduced to nearly nothing. After trying to deliver hundreds of bills and collecting nothing, one postal worker decided to stay at home the next day and paid all the bills himself for a few cents.

The worst case of hyper-inflation however, occurred in Hungary post World War II and collectable Hungarian banknotes serve as a stark reminder of the time. The record for largest denomination of circulated paper currency is, in fact, Hungary, after it printed the 100 quintillion note in 1946. 100 quintillion is a 1... with 20 zeros after it, or 100 million million million. This is what it looks like: 100,000,000,000,000,000,000. The number was never written in full on the banknotes, so it does not hold the record for most zeros ever printed on a banknote.

The honour of printing the most zeros on a circulated banknote goes to the country which had the 2nd worst case of hyper-inflation ever, Zimbabwe. This African state suffered from this extreme inflation in the 1990s soon after the government confiscated private farms from their owners. In 2009, when Zimbabwe stopped printing its currency, the highest banknote being circulated was the 100,000,000,000,000 (or 100 trillion) Zimbabwean dollar. In 2015, the government announced that the country would be dollarized, and completely run on the American dollar. Ironically, the once worthless Zimbabwean dollar, is now attracting fascination from tourists. As a result, the currency souvenir industry is booming in Zimbabwe, replacing wooden handcrafts as the must have item to take home, with the one 100 trillion Zimdollar bill selling for up to $5. Many governments have found out the hard way that printing more money to increase their existing bankrolls is definitely not the best solution to their problems. As Kin Hubbard eloquently put it, "the safe way to double your money is to fold it over once and put it in your pocket."

What is money really though? Granted, having a currency is easier to handle and more practical than bartering an orange for a pineapple for instance, but how is its worth calculated? Various systems of calculating the worth or purchasing power of money have existed throughout history. The first type of money was commodity money where the actual currency was made out of of precious metals that were the equivalent value in weight. The first coins in the United States were made from actual gold, silver and copper. Eventually, due to the impracticality of carrying around large amounts of commodity money, representative money such as banknotes were created, where the banknote paper (in itself of no intrinsic value) was backed up by the precious metals. You could have therefore exchanged a hundred dollar bill made out of paper for one hundred dollars' worth of gold. The United States moved on to a mixture of commodity and representative money with the 1900 Gold Standard Act.

If you had to open up your wallet or purse right now and pull out a note or even a coin, you would not find any commodity money or representative money, because our coins are no longer made of precious metals and neither are our notes backed by these metals anymore. The money we have today is called fiat money, which originates from the Latin fiat meaning "it shall be". This type of money requires faith in the government that the money will have value and people use this money because they believe that it is worth something, and will continue to be worth something. Basically it is worth something because the government is telling you that it is and guaranteeing that it will continue to be in the future and you must believe this for it to work! Hyper-inflation can easily occur in a system of fiat money if the government no longer can or refuses to guarantee the value of the money.

As we all know though, 21st century humans are now blessed with electronic money and in fact most money around the world exists solely in this electronic form. This form of money oddly enough, apart from being convenient, can help fight crime. Criminals cannot risk using cheques or electronic means to transfer large of amounts of money but must use cash, which is risky and not the most practical when dealing with big numbers. The United States uses the 100 dollar bill as its largest note partly for this reason and even this note's future is now being questioned. The discontinuation of the 500 euro note in the European Union is also now confirmed as a way to make criminals' lives more and more difficult. As technology becomes more and more advanced and electronics ever cheaper, there might come a time when we will not see Benjamin Franklin's face on notes anymore, with money becoming solely electronic. We are probably still a long way away from the day when a 100 dollar bill will be used as a novelty bookmark though, so for now I will just have to settle for my 100 trillion Zimbabwean note!

Chapter 19: No Pictures!

A few years ago I visited Italy, more specifically Rome, and once there took the opportunity to visit the smallest sovereign state in the whole world, the Vatican City. This half a square-kilometer state, with a population of just over 800 people, is actually within the city of Rome, surrounded by it to be precise, yet it is independent and ruled by the bishop of Rome, the head of the Roman Catholic Church... the Pope. From this ecclesiastical state, the Pope and his clergy oversee the affairs of the Catholic Church. One does not visit to see the way the Church conducts their affairs though, but to see the fantastic architecture and art that is on offer in such a small space. The St. Peter's Basilica, Vatican Museums and the Sistine Chapel can all be found in the Vatican, and it is the entrance fees and associated merchandise of these hotspots that fuels the economy of the Vatican City.

Out of all the sights I saw, and facts I learnt that day, it was the Sistine chapel's beauty and story that struck me the most. This chapel can be found in the Apostolic Palace of the Vatican, which is the Pope's official residence. It was originally called the Cappella Magna but was later named after Pope Sixtus IV who restored it in the 15th century. Entering the majestic building is an experience that I will never forget. This chapel houses some great (understatement) frescoes famously painted by Michelangelo which I was lucky enough to have seen. To explain how great these works of art truly are I should quote writer and statesman Johann Wolfgang Goethe who in 1787 said:

"Without having seen the Sistine Chapel one can form no appreciable idea of what one man is capable of achieving."

I fully agreed with that sentiment, and quickly reached for my phone to take a photo and capture this moment forever, only to be met by loud disapproval. I wondered what the reasons for this ban on photographs could be. Later that day I overheard a tour guide explain to a group that the reason why tourists cannot take photos inside the Sistine Chapel is because the copyrights to all the images of the priceless art belong to... a Japanese television network. Could that be true? It turns out, that the Japanese public broadcasting station Nippon TV or NHK was the highest bidder, at around $US 4 million, when the Vatican reached out for funds to restore the frescoes in the chapel. In exchange for this funding, NHK was granted exclusive photo and filming rights of the works in the Sistine Chapel. Restoration works started in 1980 and finished just under 20 years later, with all stages of restoration meticulously documented by the broadcasting station. This was not the last time NHK funded works of such great importance, as they also paid for the renovation of the Mona Lisa viewing room which was completed in 2015 as well as the renovation of the area in the Louvre housing Venus de Milo!

One thing the tour guide did not divulge though, was that the exclusive copyright granted to NHK was only for a limited amount of time, three years after each stage of restoration was complete to be exact. Since works were completed in 1999, then the exclusive copyrights definitely do not hold now. So why does this photography (and videography for that matter) ban still exist?

Presumably they decided to keep enforcing the ban after the copyright expired for one reason or another. Maybe they do not want flash photography, as it would harm the frescoes, and found that simply banning all photography would be much easier to control? Maybe it is a form of crowd control to avoid the congestion of amateur photographers all trying to get the best shot? Maybe it is a way of making you appreciate the art and not distract you from the experience? Or maybe it is simply a way of maximizing profit and forcing you to buy a postcard or book as you exit through the gift-shop.

Whatever the reason, I realized that us humans are beginning to live our lives through a lens rather than appreciate the moment as it unfolds before us. Even though there were multiple signs reminding everyone not to take photos and the guards repeating the words "no pictures" every couple of seconds, people around me were still trying to snap a sneaky shot of the ceiling, as some sort of trophy perhaps. The sad truth is that any photo taken, with the low lighting from their mediocre camera, would never capture the true beauty of these images that could have been appreciated with their own eyes if only they had the time to look around and admire it. They managed to walk away with their trophy though, a low-quality, dark, blurry trophy. The same trend can be seen in music concerts nowadays. Gone are the times when a whole crowd would watch a band live and simply enjoy the music. Now we have a sea of hands in the air but for the wrong reasons, holding phones and cameras taking videos of the stage, to post on social media perhaps, as a way of showing others that they were there. The video itself is terrible, out of focus, shaky, and the music nearly indistinguishable. Their experience of the concert itself? Diminished. I too have a few of these video clips somewhere (they couldn't have been too important!), but now I am trying my hardest to resist the urge to reach for the lens and simply just live in the moment!

Chapter 20: Mach 0.85

Today I woke up flying through the air at speeds of around 900 km per hour (around 560 miles per hour). Another very 21st century thing to be doing. Although this speed is quite an impressive one to be travelling at, it is still considered to be subsonic as it is less than the speed of sound. Mach is a speed measurement based on the speed of sound and as soon as you reach Mach 1 you are travelling at the speed of sound (1234.8 km per hour or 767 miles per hour). Anything Mach 1 and over and you are breaking the sound barrier, you even get a great explosion sound to prove this, called a sonic boom! (Does anybody remember Guile's sonic boom move from Capcom's Street Fighter video game?)

Passenger planes nowadays do not break the sound barrier, but that was oddly not always the case. Concorde which began service in 1976 was the first successful supersonic passenger airplane to fly (the only other supersonic passenger plane was the failed Soviet Tupolev Tu-144, which retired after only 55 passenger flights) and had a top speed of just over Mach 2, twice the speed of sound! This translates to a flight from London to New York taking just 3 and a half hours, as opposed to a bit less than double that nowadays. On April 10th 2003 both British Airways and Air France, the airlines that used Concorde, announced that they were retiring the airplane citing high maintenance costs and low passenger numbers following the 25th July 2000 Concorde crash and the September 11th attacks.

You might be pleased to find out that Airbus is working on a 20 passenger plane dubbed the Concorde 2.0, which hopes to have speeds which will more than double the original Concorde, 4.5 Mach, which would mean you could travel from London to New York in just one hour! Would this be the fastest a human has ever travelled though? Not by a long shot. Although it will probably be the most a *regular* human will be able to travel. The fastest speed humans ever travelled, astronauts to be precise, was set by the crew of Apollo 10 returning from the Moon on the 26th May 1969. The speed recorded by the mission report upon re-entry was that of 24816 miles per hour, nearly 40,000 km per hour. 32 MACH!

Most of us will probably never experience speeds of that magnitude, and I cannot say that I'm not happy about that. Until then, we will have to sit in our chairs high up in the sky travelling at measly speeds of 0.85 Mach. These sort of speeds give us more time to look around and analyse our environment, a wonder of modern engineering. As the cabin crew rushed around the plane handing out blankets, water and alcohol, I gave my surroundings a proper inspection and realized that I didn't have the answer to some things that I always took for granted.

First of all, why do airplanes have round windows? Was it a design feature to make them look super sleek or did it have some ulterior scientific motive? I assumed it would be the latter and after some research this was indeed the case. To understand why round windows are needed we would first need to understand why modern passenger planes were designed the way they are in the first place.

The first jet aircraft to be specially built for passenger travel was the de Havilland Comet in the late 1940s in Britain, and jet engines were chosen due to their speed, reliability and noise reduction. Jet engines were a novelty back then as passengers were used to noisy propeller powered aircraft, so it was a step that would surely revolutionize air travel. The only problem was that jet fuel was consumed too quickly especially at low altitudes of 10,000 feet (the normal altitude of flight back then). The decision was made to increase the altitude of travel to over 30,000 feet, triple the normal altitude as the air was thinner and therefore less power would be required. One more problem here though. The inconvenient little problem of humans not being able to breathe at that altitude! This meant the planes would need a pressurized tube-shaped cabin.

Pressurization means that while the airplane is climbing higher, air would be pumped into the cabin until the pressure is greater than the pressure outside. This enables passengers to breathe without oxygen masks and essentially not die. When the plane begins to descend during landing, cabin pressure would again have to be regulated. This cycle of expanding the tubular cabin slightly when climbing and then contracting when pressure was being released, put a great strain on the body of the plane each time it happened. Did I mention that aircrafts had rectangular windows back then? It would transpire that on a tubular designed aircraft, stress would flow easily around it only to be stopped by the sharp corners of a rectangular window causing a build-up of pressure.

Regrettably, it was not until a series of Comet crashes that were attributed specifically to the window shape that a redesign was needed. Upon testing other Comets on land, crash investigators found that the most pressure was in fact exerted at the corners of these rectangular windows making the planes susceptible to breaking up under this stress. The findings of this crash investigation changed airline history forever. American aircraft production in the form of Boeing took the lead from de Havilland which never recovered and of course all future aircraft windows were designed with round windows and remained that way until today. Round windows on a tubular aircraft therefore do not cause any interruption in flow.

You might be asking, what is that tiny hole found in all airplane windows used for though? Observant human. This hole, known technically as a breather hole or bleed hole, is also linked with pressure. This little hole is there for pressurization and since an airplane window has more than one layer, the inside window needs to be equalized. Typically an airplane window would have 3 different panes, the inner, the middle and the outer, which are all made of an extremely strong synthetic material rather than glass. The hole is usually found in the middle window pane and the outer and middle windows are actually structural whereas the inner window is there to protect the other panes. The outer pane is the primary structural window and bears the stress of pressurization in typical circumstances. The hole serves as a valve, ensuring cabin pressure is only applied to the outer pane during the flight.

It is not strange to sometimes notice ice particles around the hole, and this is due to the air in between the windows being much colder than the cabin air. The breather hole also draws moisture out that gets trapped between the panes, keeping it mist free and allowing you to enjoy the view.

Speaking of views, why are we forced to look at those spectacular views below the plane by having to leave the window shades open during take-off and landing? It turns out that there are a handful of reasons for this. The main reason is that the crew is preparing the plane for any possible emergency since they have a time frame of

90 seconds to evacuate passengers. Apart from opening window shades, they would also inform you to stow your tray table away and put your seat in an upright position. The last two would enable you to manoeuvre better in an emergency, whereas the opening of window shades would allow the crew to analyse the outside better and come up with an appropriate evacuation plan. Other reasons are that during take-off and landing (the most crucial stages of the flight), passengers can look out and immediately alert crew of any unfortunate activity such as an engine failure. The shades open during the day would also allow the passengers eyes to adjust to the light, whilst during take-off and landing during night time the cabin lights dim, adjusting the passengers eyes to low light in case of any emergency. I guess they weren't trying to set the mood by dimming the lights after all!

Chapter 21: What Came First, The Chicken Or The Egg?

The 'chicken or the egg?' dilemma has been around for quite a while now, longer than one might imagine. The Greek philosopher Aristotle in the 4th century BC was fascinated by this question and concluded that both must have existed at the same time, as he was of the belief that everything that was born on our planet must have, at some point, existed before in spirit form. Another Greek thinker, Plutarch, specifically mentioned a hen in his discussions. Although never giving an answer, he acknowledges that by posing this question one would be opening up to an even bigger question, that of the creation of the world. These ancient thinkers however, did not yet understand what we call evolution nowadays, because if they did they might have been able to answer the question a little bit better.

First of all, a quick recap of why we have this dilemma. We all know that a chicken is needed to lay an egg and we all know that an egg is needed to create a chicken. This is the cycle that causes so much grief and the dilemma that ensues is trying to find some cut off point in this cycle by which we can give a definite answer. As we will soon find out, there is an answer or answers rather, depending on how you look at the question.

What came first, the chicken or the egg? OK. Are we talking about ANY type of egg or an actual chicken egg? If we are referring to any egg then the answer would definitely be egg, as eggs existed way before chickens did. Dinosaurs laid eggs and dinosaurs were around far longer than chickens were. So maybe the question should really be, "What came first, the chicken or the chicken egg?" Here is where the answer gets a little trickier.

It is important to understand at this point that the chicken (gallus gallus domesticus) evolved from other birds to become the animal that we know today. It is actually a direct descendant of the red jungle fowl of Thailand, which is said to be the ancestor from which all domestic chickens that exist originated from. So at some point in time there was of course a first chicken, however the parents of that chicken, that is, the female who laid the egg and the male who fertilized it, were not chickens themselves. Let us call these parents "almost-chickens". So these almost-chickens created the first chicken and the chicken entered the world in the same way chickens do today, in an egg.

Here is the tricky part though. Would you call the egg that was laid by these almost-chickens a chicken egg, on the merit of it containing a chicken? Or would you call it an almost-chicken egg because it was laid by an almost-chicken. Choosing one over the other would produce different answers to our age old question. If you consider the egg a chicken egg, then our answer would therefore be egg, however if you consider it an almost-chicken egg then since the egg is not a chicken egg, the chicken would come first. In my opinion, although both arguments do have points, I would tend to say that an egg should be classified by what it contains and not who lays it. If cats and dog had to lay eggs and a dog laid an egg from which a cat hatched, I would say that it was a cat egg rather than a dog egg. To conclude therefore, I believe the answer is egg because two birds (almost-chickens) created the first chicken egg which then became the first chicken. All this talk made me hungry. Does anybody else think it's weird to eat chicken and eggs together? The Japanese even have a chicken and egg dish called Oyakodon, which literally translates to 'the parent and child bowl.' Humans really are strange!

Quiz Questions

(Answers can be found in the page directly after these 30 questions)

Q1. What colour of clothing did most children wear before cheap dyes were invented?

Q2. What sign did the Nazis put on homosexual men when they thought they could be 'cured' from their ways?

Q3. What sacred Hindu and Buddhist symbol became associated with evil due to World War II?

Q4. What is the fear of flying called?

Q5. What is the term given to turbulence that airplanes leave behind them, which could disturb other airplanes in their path?

Q6. What is the proper term for a bird colliding with an airplane?

Q7. What hormone does the pancreas produce to regulate your blood sugar level?

Q8. An abjad is an alphabet that lacks what?

Q9. Who was the cursive writing, known as Carolingian miniscule, named after?

Q10. What do you call a phrase that uses all the letters of the alphabet at least once?

Q11. How would you say the word 'RAMBLINGS' using the NATO phonetic alphabet?

Q12. What food is the most popular of Italy's dishes?

Q13. What two pizzas are considered the only two true Neapolitan pizzas?

Q14. What phenomenon makes a stick look like it is broken when it is put into water?

Q15. According to legend, what did Saint Dunstan hammer into the Devil, which now became a symbol for good luck?

Q16. Find the only true nut out of these: almond, hazelnut, walnut, cashew nut, peanut

Q17. Who invented the first printing press?

Q18. What is AT&T an abbreviation for?

Q19. Who is the 3rd month of the year named after?

Q20. Was the year 2000 a leap year?

Q21. Which Norse god is the day directly following Wednesday, named after?

Q22. What day do Italians fear, rather than Friday the 13th?

Q23. What animal's head is the letter 'A' based on?

Q24. What language does the word Aardvark come from?

Q25. What is the capital city of Armenia?

Q26. How many zeros does 1 quintillion have in it?

Q27. What is the smallest sovereign state in the world?

Q28. What do you call the loud sound that is heard after breaking the sound barrier?

Q29. Which American aircraft producer took the lead from the British after a series of British plane crashes?

Q30. What common domesticated animal is a direct descendant of the red jungle fowl of Thailand?

Quiz Answers

A1. White

A2. A pink triangle

A3. The swastika

A4. Aviophobia or aerophobia

A5. Wake turbulence

A6. Bird strike

A7. Insulin

A8. Vowels

A9. Emperor Charlemagne

A10. A pangram

A11. Romeo Alpha Mike Bravo Lima India November Golf Sierra

A12. Pasta

A13. The pizza marinara and the pizza Margherita

A14. Refraction

A15. A horse-shoe

A16. Hazelnut

A17. Johannes Gutenburg

A18. The American Telephone and Telegraph Company

A19. Mars, the god of war

A20. Yes. Even though it is divisible by 100, it is divisible by 400.

A21. Thor

A22. Friday the 17th

A23. Ox

A24. Afrikaans

A25. Yerevan

A26. 18

A27. The Vatican City

A28. A sonic boom

A29. Boeing

A30. Chicken

Conclusion

I sincerely hope you enjoyed the first book in the series. You could say that the future of *Ramblings of a 21st Century Human* is literally in your hands. Once again, I would really appreciate it if you could leave a review and also spread the word with your human friends (animal friends too if necessary). Even though I am currently working on the second book in the series, the response and feedback to this first one will obviously give me a better idea as to where I stand.

Thank you.

I.M. Human

Sources and Further Reading

Chapter 1

http://news.bbc.co.uk/2/hi/uk_news/magazine/7817496.stm

http://www.smithsonianmag.com/arts-culture/when-did-girls-start-wearing-pink-1370097/

http://hollowbranch.blogspot.com.mt/2015/01/girls-wear-pink-boys-wear-blue.html

http://www.fastcodesign.com/1672751/how-pink-and-blue-became-gender-specific

http://www.npr.org/2014/04/01/297159948/girls-are-taught-to-think-pink-but-that-wasnt-always-so

http://people.howstuffworks.com/gender-color.htm

http://jezebel.com/5790638/the-history-of-pink-for-girls-blue-for-boys

http://www.theatlantic.com/entertainment/archive/2015/04/when-unisex-was-the-new-black/390168/

http://historywired.si.edu/detail.cfm?ID=119

https://en.wikipedia.org/wiki/Swastika

http://wackulus.com/ou-wont-believe-just-find-swastika-world-war-ii/

http://www.bbc.com/news/magazine-29644591

http://www.nytimes.com/library/arts/072900tank-swastika.html

http://theweek.com/articles/456370/no-swastika-cant-rehabilitated

http://www.latimes.com/opinion/opinion-la/la-ol-swastika-fashion-carlsberg-20140814-story.html

https://en.wikipedia.org/wiki/Toothbrush_moustache

http://www.bbc.co.uk/nottingham/content/articles/2009/07/16/john_peake_knight_traffic_lights_feature.shtml

http://www.bmoperators.com/?p=492

http://cdnc.ucr.edu/cgi-bin/cdnc?a=d&d=SFC19111216.2.181.15.3

https://en.wikipedia.org/wiki/Traffic_light

http://jalopnik.com/how-traffic-lights-came-to-be-and-why-green-means-go-1763294225

http://www.wired.com/2014/02/throwback-thursday-sweden/

https://en.wikipedia.org/wiki/Dagen_H

Chapter 2

https://www.flightradar24.com/

http://flightaware.com/

https://planefinder.net/

http://www.techinsider.io/flight-radar-planes-2015-8

http://gizmodo.com/5962727/this-insane-image-shows-how-many-planes-are-in-the-air-right-now-for-thanksgiving

http://www.smithsonianmag.com/smart-news/a-map-of-every-passenger-plane-in-the-skies-at-this-instant-39070996/

http://www.theblaze.com/stories/2012/09/18/see-what-more-than-6000-planes-flying-worldwide-at-one-time-looks-like/

http://sos.noaa.gov/Datasets/dataset.php?id=44

http://www.atag.org/facts-and-figures.html

www.statisticbrain.com/airplane-crash-statistics/

http://www.planecrashinfo.com/cause.htm

http://www.cnbc.com/2014/12/30/despite-fatal-airline-crash-statistics-flying-is-still-safe.html

http://elitedaily.com/news/world/people-terrified-plane-crashes-even-though-rare/977885/

http://anxieties.com/flying-howsafe.php#.VzGY_oR97IV

http://www.channel4.com/programmes/the-plane-crash/articles/all/plane-crash-facts

http://www.iii.org/fact-statistic/mortality-risk

http://www.livescience.com/3780-odds-dying.html

http://www.besthealthdegrees.com/health-risks/

http://edition.cnn.com/2015/02/06/travel/plane-crash-survival-tips-feat/

https://en.wikipedia.org/wiki/Fear_of_flying

http://abcnews.go.com/International/odds-surviving-plane-crash/story?id=22886654

http://edition.cnn.com/interactive/2014/07/travel/aviation-data/

http://www.turbulenceforecast.com/

http://www.askthepilot.com/questionanswers/turbulence/

http://www.telegraph.co.uk/travel/travel-truths/What-causes-turbulence-and-is-it-dangerous/

http://www.livescience.com/43448-air-turbulence-dangerous-injuries.html

http://fearofflyingschool.com/airplane-turbulence

http://www.cbc.ca/news/technology/turbulence-air-travel-1.3385566

http://www.metoffice.gov.uk/learning/wind/what-is-the-jet-stream

http://skepticalscience.com/jetstream-guide.html

http://www.skybrary.aero/index.php/Mitigation_of_Wake_Turbulence_Hazard

http://www.eurocontrol.int/articles/wake-vortex

http://www.askcaptainlim.com/air-turbulence-weather-58/1156-hurt-by-wake-turbulence.html

http://www.slate.com/articles/news_and_politics/explainer/2012/06/can_turbulence_cause_a_plane_crash_.html

http://www.latimes.com/business/la-fi-airline-turbulence-injuries-rare-20141226-story.html

http://www.bbc.com/future/story/20140319-stress-tests-for-safer-planes

http://www.snopes.com/science/cannon.asp

http://www.popularmechanics.com/flight/g2428/7-airplane-wing-stress-tests/

http://www.askcaptainlim.com/air-turbulence-weather-58/850-what-i-fear-about-flying-is-the-stomach-sinking-feeling.html

http://usatoday30.usatoday.com/travel/columnist/getline/2005-10-03-ask-the-captain_x.htm

http://www.foxnews.com/travel/2014/05/05/demystifying-flying-what-is-air-pocket.html

http://www.airliners.net/aviation-forums/general_aviation/print.main?id=1301544

http://www.usatoday.com/story/travel/columnist/cox/2012/11/05/ask-the-captain-in-flight-chimes-cabin-temperature-feedback/1682735/

Chapter 3

http://www.ucsusa.org/center-science-and-democracy/added-sugar-nutrition-facts-label

http://www.heart.org/HEARTORG/HealthyLiving/HealthyEating/Nutrition/Sugar-101_UCM_306024_Article.jsp

http://www.scientificamerican.com/article/should-added-sugar-be-on-the-nutrition-facts-labels/

http://www.choosemyplate.gov/what-are-added-sugars

http://www.newhealthguide.org/How-Many-Grams-Of-Sugar-In-A-Teaspoon.html

https://en.wikipedia.org/wiki/Added_sugar

http://familydoctor.org/familydoctor/en/prevention-wellness/food-nutrition/sugar-and-substitutes/added-sugar-what-you-need-to-know.html

http://www.hsph.harvard.edu/nutritionsource/carbohydrates/added-sugar-in-the-diet/

https://en.wikipedia.org/wiki/Empty_calorie

http://www.alternet.org/food/9-shocking-facts-you-need-know-about-sugar

http://www.forbes.com/sites/alicegwalton/2012/08/30/how-much-sugar-are-americans-eating-infographic/

http://www.health.harvard.edu/blog/eating-too-much-added-sugar-increases-the-risk-of-dying-with-heart-disease-201402067021

https://www.diabetes.org.uk/Guide-to-diabetes/Enjoy-food/Food-shopping-for-diabetes/Understanding-food-labels/

http://www.womhealth.org.au/healthy-lifestyle/food-labels-what-they-really-mean

http://www.calculator.net/calorie-calculator.html

https://www.ted.com/talks/jamie_oliver?language=en

http://www.whfoods.com/genpage.php?tname=faq&dbid=32

http://www.nidcr.nih.gov/DataStatistics/FindDataByTopic/Dental Caries/DentalCariesAdults20to64.htm

http://time.com/3380563/sugar-tooth-decay/

http://edition.cnn.com/2015/10/04/health/roman-sugar-healthy-teeth/

http://www.forbes.com/sites/jacobsullum/2013/10/16/research-shows-cocaine-and-heroin-are-less-addictive-than-oreos/

http://www.webmd.com/food-recipes/your-brain-on-sugar

CHAPTER 4

http://www.history.com/news/ask-history/who-created-the-first-alphabet

http://www.ancient.eu/alphabet/

http://www.usu.edu/markdamen/1320hist&civ/pp/slides/17alphabet.pdf

http://fluentfocus.com/the-history-of-the-english-alphabet/

http://www.citrinitas.com/history_of_viscom/alphabet.html

https://en.wikipedia.org/wiki/History_of_the_alphabet

https://doyoukno.wordpress.com/2008/10/19/the-origins-and-history-of-the-alphabet/

http://www.omniglot.com/writing/protosinaitc.htm

http://www.ancientscripts.com/protosinaitic.html

https://en.wikipedia.org/wiki/Abjad

https://en.wikipedia.org/wiki/Phoenician_alphabet

http://i.imgur.com/FyVXx.gif

http://terpconnect.umd.edu/~rfradkin/latin.html

http://www.oxforddictionaries.com/words/why-is-the-alphabet-arranged-the-way-it-is

https://en.wikipedia.org/wiki/Alphabetical_order

https://twitter.com/neiltyson/status/259486092766625793

http://www.todayifoundout.com/index.php/2011/02/where-upper-case-and-lower-case-came-from/

http://www.britannica.com/art/Carolingian-minuscule

http://clagnut.com/blog/2380/

http://www.fun-with-words.com/pangrams.html

https://www.google.com.mt/search?q=anagram

https://en.wikipedia.org/wiki/Palindrome

http://www.palindromelist.net/

http://www.omniglot.com/writing/morsecode.htm

http://morsecode.scphillips.com/morse2.html

https://en.wikipedia.org/wiki/Braille

http://www.alphabravocharlie.info/alphabet.php

Chapter 5

http://www.bbc.com/news/magazine-13760559

http://www.bbc.co.uk/food/0/20515123

http://www.passion-4-pizza.com/italian_pizza.html

https://en.wikipedia.org/wiki/History_of_pizza

http://slice.seriouseats.com/archives/2013/01/serious-eats-guide-to-eating-pizza-in-naples-napoli-italy-neapolitan-pizza.html

http://pizza.com/chicago-style-pizza-vs-new-york-style-pizza

http://www.passion-4-pizza.com/new_york_pizza.html

http://www.bbc.com/travel/story/20131023-the-deep-rooted-history-of-chicagos-deep-dish-pizza

http://articles.chicagotribune.com/2009-02-18/news/0902180055_1_chicago-pizza-ric-riccardo-pizzeria-uno

https://www.fornobravo.com/pizzaquest/2011/11/15/the-marinara/

http://www.silviocicchi.com/pizzachef/la-pizza-marinara-ricetta-e-preparazione/?lang=en

http://www.lifeinitaly.com/food/pizza-margherita-naples

http://www.lifeinitaly.com/food/pizza-history.asp

http://www.pizzanapoletana.org/

http://www.pizzanapoletana.org/public/pdf/disciplinare%202008%20UK.pdf

Chapter 6

http://www.mrc-cbu.cam.ac.uk/people/matt.davis/cmabridge/

https://en.wikipedia.org/wiki/Typoglycemia

http://www.archimedes-lab.org/what_is_illusion.html

http://www.buzzle.com/articles/history-of-optical-illusions.html

http://mercercognitivepsychology.pbworks.com/w/page/612072 70/Perceptual%20Illusions

http://www.opticalspy.com/spy-blog/a-brief-history-of-optical-illusions

http://ist-socrates.berkeley.edu/~kihlstrm/JastrowDuck.htm

http://io9.gizmodo.com/the-worlds-most-famous-and-ambiguous-illusion-1646895274

http://psylux.psych.tu-dresden.de/i1/kaw/diverses%20Material/www.illusionworks.com /html/perceptual_ambiguity.html

http://mathworld.wolfram.com/YoungGirl-OldWomanIllusion.html

http://espejo-ludico.blogspot.com.mt/2011/11/la-verdadera-historia-de-la-mujer-joven.html

http://mathworld.wolfram.com/Rabbit-DuckIllusion.html

Chapter 7

http://www.crystalwind.ca/eureka-amazing/ancient-wisdom/superstitions/the-lucky-penny

http://goodlucksymbols.com/

http://www.thinkmoney.co.uk/news-advice/top-ten-money-superstitions-0-4220-0.htm

http://www.thepursuitofgreen.com/2013/12/16/picking-up-pennies-nickels-and-dimes/

http://www.mindblowing-facts.org/2013/02/finding-pennies-is-considered-good-luck-because-years-ago-people-thought-that-finding-metal-was-a-gift-from-the-gods-and-meant-to-protect-you-from-evil/

http://blogs.scientificamerican.com/anthropology-in-practice/what-makes-a-rabbits-foot-lucky/

https://en.wikipedia.org/wiki/Rabbit%27s_foot

http://www.luckymojo.com/rabbitfoot.html

http://boingboing.net/2011/10/26/why-are-rabbits-feet-considered-lucky.html

http://www.unexplainedstuff.com/Superstitions-Strange-Customs-Taboos-and-Urban-Legends/Superstitions-Rabbit-s-foot.html

https://www.mirrorservice.org/sites/gutenberg.org/1/3/9/7/13978/13978-h/13978-h.htm

http://www.csicop.org/superstition/library/horseshoes

http://psychiclibrary.com/beyondBooks/horseshoe-superstition/

http://goodlucksymbols.com/good-luck-horseshoe/

http://www.luckymojo.com/horseshoe.html

http://superstitionsonline.com/horseshoe-superstitions-good-luck-up-and-down/

http://goodlucksymbols.com/wishbone-luck/

http://people.howstuffworks.com/wishbones-lucky.htm

http://www.luckymojo.com/wishbone.html

http://goodlucksymbols.com/elephants/

http://www.elephantsforever.co.za/the-elephant-charm.html

http://www.luckymojo.com/elephant.html

http://goodlucksymbols.com/tortoise-symbolism/

http://animal-world.com/newsfeed/frog-luck-bringing-changes-abundance-life/

http://www.whats-your-sign.com/animal-symbolism-frog.html

http://goodlucksymbols.com/good-luck-frog/

https://en.wikipedia.org/wiki/Jin_Chan

http://www.lifedeathprizes.com/amazing-stuff/abracadabra-lucky-charm-ward-off-misfortune-1769

http://www.luckymojo.com/willss13abracadabra.html

http://psychiclibrary.com/beyondBooks/four-leaf-clover-superstition/

http://goodlucksymbols.com/four-leaf-clover/

http://www.lucky-four-leaf-clover.com/what.html

http://www.irishcentral.com/roots/history/Where-does-the-term-the-luck-of-the-Irish-come-from.html

http://www.theemeraldisle.org/irish-sayings/luck-of-the-irish.htm

Chapter 8

https://en.wikipedia.org/wiki/List_of_culinary_nuts

https://en.wikipedia.org/wiki/Nut_(fruit)

http://www.telegraph.co.uk/men/the-filter/qi/8434868/QI-Quite-interesting-facts-about-nuts.html

http://www.newworldencyclopedia.org/entry/Nut

http://healthimpactnews.com/2014/how-did-almonds-surpass-peanuts-as-americas-top-nut-the-dark-side-of-almonds/

http://www.todayifoundout.com/index.php/2012/05/california-produces-about-80-of-the-almonds-in-the-world/

http://www.thewire.com/national/2014/07/almonds-are-sucking-the-life-out-of-california/374373/

http://www.npr.org/sections/thesalt/2015/04/16/399958203/how-almonds-became-a-scapegoat-for-californias-drought

https://en.wikipedia.org/wiki/Drupe

http://www.seriouseats.com/2010/04/what-are-the-differences-between-nuts-and-drupes.html

http://knowledgenuts.com/2013/12/22/difference-between-nuts-legumes-and-drupes/

http://www.peanut-institute.org/peanut-facts/

http://www.whfoods.com/genpage.php?tname=foodspice&dbid=101

https://en.wikipedia.org/wiki/Brazil_nut

http://www.nutrition-and-you.com/brazil-nuts.html

https://en.wikipedia.org/wiki/Macadamia

http://www.nutrition-and-you.com/macadamia-nut.html

https://en.wikipedia.org/wiki/Pine_nut

http://www.diffen.com/difference/Angiosperms_vs_Gymnosperms

http://www.whfoods.com/genpage.php?tname=foodspice&dbid=98

http://www.evilmadscientist.com/2007/cashews-the-nut-you-cant-buy-in-a-shell/

http://content.time.com/time/world/article/0,8599,2092004,00.html

Chapter 10

http://www.shadycharacters.co.uk/series/the-ampersand/

https://designshack.net/articles/typography/why-i-love-ampersands-you-should-too/

http://blog.dictionary.com/ampersand/

http://www.fastcodesign.com/3055622/why-designers-love-the-ampersand

http://www.webdesignerdepot.com/2010/01/the-history-of-the-ampersand-and-showcase/

http://www.oxforddictionaries.com/words/origin-of-ampersand

http://www.newyorker.com/books/page-turner/the-ancient-roots-of-punctuation

http://www.artlebedev.com/mandership/112/

https://en.wikipedia.org/wiki/Ampersand

http://www.uh.edu/~mbarber/mondegreens.html

http://www.newyorker.com/science/maria-konnikova/science-misheard-lyrics-mondegreens

http://www.fun-with-words.com/mala_mondegreens.html

http://etc.usf.edu/lit2go/74/nursery-rhymes-and-traditional-poems/3039/a-was-an-apple-pie/

https://en.wikipedia.org/wiki/Apple_Pie_ABC

http://www.wga.org/content/default.aspx?id=1019#credits4

Chapter 11

http://www.huffingtonpost.com/2012/01/30/babylonian-yo-mama-joke_n_1242617.html

https://www.scripted.com/content-marketing-2/yo-mama-joke-history/

http://io9.gizmodo.com/5880232/the-worlds-oldest-yo-mama-joke-is-3500-years-old

https://en.wikipedia.org/wiki/Maternal_insult

http://knowyourmeme.com/memes/your-mom-jokes

https://en.wikipedia.org/wiki/The_Dozens

http://www.elijahwald.com/dozens.html

http://www.humorsearch.com/humor/yo-mama-jokes.html

http://www.jokes4us.com/yomamajokes/index.html

Chapter 12

http://www.kelsung.com/calendar.htm

http://www.freetech4teachers.com/2012/02/history-of-calendars-leap-year-and.html

http://www.infoplease.com/ipa/A0002061.html

http://www.infoplease.com/calendar/lunar.html

https://en.wikipedia.org/wiki/History_of_calendars

http://www.timekeepingsite.org/calendar.htm

https://en.wikipedia.org/wiki/Roman_calendar

http://www.timeanddate.com/calendar/roman-calendar.html

http://www.timeanddate.com/calendar/julian-gregorian-switch.html

http://libguides.ctstatelibrary.org/hg/colonialresearch/calendar

http://www.windhorst.org/calendar/

https://en.wikipedia.org/wiki/French_Republican_Calendar

http://www.webexhibits.org/calendars/calendar-french.html

http://www.tondering.dk/claus/cal/french.php

http://www.britannica.com/science/French-republican-calendar

http://history1900s.about.com/od/1920s/a/sovietcalendar.htm

https://en.wikipedia.org/wiki/Soviet_calendar

https://www.almanac.com/content/why-week-has-seven-days

http://www.webexhibits.org/calendars/week.html

http://hansard.millbanksystems.com/commons/1944/mar/17/calendar-reform

http://www.timekeepingsite.org/clock_invent.html

http://www.scientificamerican.com/article/experts-time-division-days-hours-minutes/

http://www.historyworld.net/wrldhis/PlainTextHistories.asp?historyid=191

http://www.livescience.com/44964-why-60-minutes-in-an-hour.html

https://traveltoeat.com/french-revolution-decimal-watches/

http://io9.gizmodo.com/5886129/the-short-strange-history-of-decimal-time

http://www-groups.dcs.st-and.ac.uk/history/HistTopics/Decimal_time.html

https://en.wikipedia.org/wiki/Decimal_time

http://physics.nist.gov/cuu/Units/second.html

http://www.scientificamerican.com/article/how-does-one-arrive-at-th/

http://www.astronomynotes.com/gravappl/s10.htm

http://tycho.usno.navy.mil/leapsec.html

https://en.wikipedia.org/wiki/Tidal_acceleration

http://www.timeanddate.com/time/time-zones-history.html

http://www.worldtimeserver.com/learn/history-of-time-zones/

http://news.nationalgeographic.com/news/2015/03/150306-daylight-savings-time-spring-forward-united-states-science-nation/

http://www.timeanddate.com/time/dst/history.html

http://www.timeanddate.com/time/dst/daylight-saving-debate.html

http://www.bls.gov/tus/charts/

http://www.wsj.com/articles/sleep-experts-close-in-on-the-optimal-nights-sleep-1405984970

http://distractify.com/old-school/2015/01/07/astounding-facts-about-how-we-actually-spend-our-time-1197818577

Chapter 13

http://www.merriam-webster.com/dictionary/triskaidekaphobia

http://mathworld.wolfram.com/Triskaidekaphobia.html

https://en.wikipedia.org/wiki/Triskaidekaphobia

http://time.com/3708916/friday-the-13th/

http://www.theparisreview.org/blog/2015/03/13/morituri-te-salutamus/

https://en.wikipedia.org/wiki/Friday_the_13th

http://news.nationalgeographic.com/news/2004/02/0212_04021
2_friday13.html

http://www.ibtimes.com/friday-13th-history-origins-myths-superstitions-unlucky-day-395108

http://www.csicop.org/superstition/library/mirrors

http://www.mirrorhistory.com/mirror-facts/broken-mirror/

http://www.wisegeek.org/why-is-it-considered-bad-luck-to-break-a-mirror.htm

http://psychiclibrary.com/beyondBooks/broken-mirror-superstition/

http://www.wisegeek.org/why-is-it-considered-bad-luck-to-walk-under-a-ladder.htm

http://www.timelessmyths.co.uk/walking-under-a-ladder.html

http://psychiclibrary.com/beyondBooks/ladder-superstition/

http://www.csicop.org/superstition/library/umbrellas

http://psychiclibrary.com/beyondBooks/umbrella-superstition/

https://en.wikipedia.org/wiki/Black_cat

http://www.timelessmyths.co.uk/a-black-cat-crossing-your-path.html

http://www.csicop.org/superstition/library/black_cats

Chapter 15

http://blog.dictionary.com/a/

http://ancienthistory.about.com/od/language/a/A.htm

https://en.wikipedia.org/wiki/Alpha

https://en.wikipedia.org/wiki/A

http://www.merriam-webster.com/dictionary/allograph

http://www.oxforddictionaries.com/words/which-letters-are-used-most

https://en.wikipedia.org/wiki/Aardvark

http://animals.nationalgeographic.com/animals/mammals/aardvark/

http://www.forbes.com/2005/04/19/cz_rk_0419karlgaard.html

http://www.skyscanner.net/news/6-best-places-see-northern-lights-winter-2015-2016

http://www.space.com/15139-northern-lights-auroras-earth-facts-sdcmp.html

http://hubpages.com/travel/The-Five-Best-Places-To-See-The-Southern-Lights-Aurora-Australis

http://www.northernlightscenter.ca/northernlights.html

http://www.pcmag.com/encyclopedia/term/37701/amara-s-law

http://www.auburn.edu/~vestmon/robotics.html

https://en.wikipedia.org/wiki/Three_Laws_of_Robotics

http://people.wku.edu/charles.smith/biogeog/ALLE1877.htm

http://www.unl.edu/rhames/courses/ppoint/heat-110.pdf

http://www.rmastudies.org.nz/documents/AbileneParadoxJerryHarvey.pdf

http://onstrategyhq.com/resources/how-to-identify-groupthink-an-introduction-to-the-abilene-paradox/

http://onstrategyhq.com/resources/how-to-avoid-bad-decisions-and-why-not-to-go-to-abilene/

http://ucavo.ucr.edu/General/Answers.html

http://www.californiaavocado.com/how-tos/your-own-avocado-tree

http://www.simplypsychology.org/asch-conformity.html

https://www.scientificamerican.com/article/milgram-nationality-conformity/

https://en.wikipedia.org/wiki/Asch_conformity_experiments

Chapter 16

http://www.encyclopedia.com/article-1G2-2831100018/board-games.html

http://www.ancientfacts.net/7-most-amazing-board-games-of-the-ancient-world/

https://en.wikipedia.org/wiki/History_of_games

http://www.cs.jhu.edu/~jorgev/cs106/ttt.pdf

http://www.chessandpoker.com/tic_tac_toe_strategy.html

http://hubpages.com/games-hobbies/Winning-Strategies-for-Connect-4-or-Four-in-a-Line-Games

http://arxiv.org/pdf/1301.3238.pdf

http://www.theatlantic.com/entertainment/archive/2015/12/how-rock-paper-scissors-went-viral/418455/

https://flowingdata.com/2010/07/30/how-to-win-rock-paper-scissors-every-time/

http://www.nytimes.com/interactive/science/rock-paper-scissors.html

http://www.wsj.com/articles/SB111473282644020271

http://worldrps.com/

http://www.nytimes.com/2005/04/29/arts/design/rock-paper-payoff-childs-play-wins-auction-house-an-art-sale.html

https://en.wikipedia.org/wiki/Rock-paper-scissors

http://www.cc.com/jokes/tqd4hj/stand-up-demetri-martin--demetri-martin--rock--paper--scissors

Chapter 17

http://www.slate.com/articles/news_and_politics/explainer/2010/10/when_did_blondes_get_so_dumb.html

http://www.academia.edu/5698808/The_Dumb_Blonde

http://www.stuffmomnevertoldyou.com/blog/historys-original-dumb-blonde/

http://www.forbes.com/sites/alicegwalton/2014/06/02/science-shatters-the-blondes-are-dumb-stereotype/

https://news.osu.edu/news/2016/03/21/blond-intelligence/

http://www.independent.co.uk/news/science/blonde-hair-intelligence-scientific-study-a6945911.html

http://www.i-c-r.org.uk/publications/monographarchive/Monograph47.pdf

http://www.lotsofjokes.com/blonde_jokes.asp

https://en.wikipedia.org/wiki/Blonde_stereotype

Chapter 18

http://www.investopedia.com/university/inflation/inflation1.asp

http://www.investopedia.com/terms/i/inflation.asp

http://www.econlib.org/library/Topics/College/supplyanddemand.html

https://simple.wikipedia.org/wiki/Supply_and_demand

http://www.economicshelp.org/blog/634/economics/the-problem-with-printing-money/

http://www.thinkinginanutshell.com/why-don-t-they-just-print-more-money

http://www.whatitcosts.com/ford-model-t-cost-prices/

http://inflationdata.com/Inflation/Inflation_Rate/Long_Term_Inflation.asp

http://www.pbs.org/wgbh/commandingheights/shared/minitext/ess_germanhyperinflation.html

https://en.wikipedia.org/wiki/Hyperinflation

http://alphahistory.com/weimarrepublic/1923-hyperinflation/

https://en.wikipedia.org/wiki/Hyperinflation_in_the_Weimar_Republic

http://www.rogershermansociety.org/yugoslavia.htm

http://www.inflation.eu/inflation-rates/hungary/historic-inflation/cpi-inflation-hungary.aspx

https://www.globalfinancialdata.com/gfdblog/?p=2382

https://en.wikipedia.org/wiki/Hungarian_peng%C5%91

https://www.rt.com/business/267244-zimbabwe-currency-compensation-hyperinflation/

http://www.telegraph.co.uk/news/worldnews/africaandindianocean/zimbabwe/3167379/Zimbabwe-inflation-hits-231-million-per-cent.html

http://www.nytimes.com/2006/05/02/world/africa/02zimbabwe.html

https://medium.com/african-makers/my-brother-went-to-zimbabwe-and-all-he-got-me-was-100-trillion-dollars-1b94cf1916b7

http://www.economist.com/news/finance-and-economics/21576665-grubby-greenbacks-dear-credit-full-shops-and-empty-factories-dollars-they

https://www.washingtonpost.com/news/wonk/wp/2015/06/12/zimbabwe-is-paying-people-5-for-175-quadrillion-zimbabwe-dollars/

http://www.investopedia.com/articles/economics/10/history-of-us-coinage.asp

http://thismatter.com/money/banking/money.htm

http://www.coins.nd.edu/ColCoin/ColCoinIntros/Commodity.intro.html

http://www.forbes.com/sites/pascalemmanuelgobry/2013/01/08/all-money-is-fiat-money/#5a9f7f5b61e5

http://neweconomicperspectives.org/2013/01/the-strange-reality-of-fiat-money.html

https://en.wikipedia.org/wiki/Fiat_money

http://time.com/money/4226174/kill-100-dollar-bill-500-euro-phase-out/

http://www.nytimes.com/2016/05/05/business/international/ecb-to-remove-500-bill-the-bin-laden-bank-note-criminals.html

https://www.occrp.org/en/daily/5213-europe-to-stop-printing-500-euro-banknote

Chapter 19

http://www.vaticanstate.va/content/vaticanstate/en/stato-e-governo/note-generali/popolazione.html

http://whc.unesco.org/en/list/286

https://en.wikipedia.org/wiki/Vatican_City

http://mentalfloss.com/article/54641/reason-why-no-photography-allowed-sistine-chapel

http://www.nytimes.com/1990/03/29/arts/nippon-tv-and-vatican.html

http://www.britannica.com/topic/restoration-of-the-ceiling-of-the-Sistine-Chapel-1324351

http://www.theregister.co.uk/2007/12/27/how_to_copyright_michelangelo/

https://portfolio.id/2013/03/why-arent-we-allowed-to-take-photographs-at-the-sistine-chapel/

https://en.wikipedia.org/wiki/Restoration_of_the_Sistine_Chapel_frescoes

CHAPTER 20

https://www.grc.nasa.gov/www/k-12/airplane/mach.html

https://www.grc.nasa.gov/www/k-12/airplane/lowsub.html

http://www.nasa.gov/audience/forstudents/k-4/stories/nasa-knows/what-is-supersonic-flight-k4.html

http://www.livescience.com/37022-speed-of-sound-mach-1.html

https://en.wikipedia.org/wiki/Mach_number

http://www.britannica.com/technology/Concorde

http://www.theatlantic.com/technology/archive/2015/07/supersonic-airplanes-concorde/396698/

https://www.museumofflight.org/aircraft/concorde

http://edition.cnn.com/2015/09/21/travel/concorde-return-to-flight/

http://www.iflscience.com/technology/new-concorde-could-fly-london-new-york-55-minutes

http://www.bbc.com/news/technology-33786999

http://www.primermagazine.com/2009/field-manual/know-it-all-what%E2%80%99s-the-fastest-speed-ever-achieved-by-a-human-being

http://history.nasa.gov/SP-4029/Apollo_10a_Summary.htm

http://www.smithsonianmag.com/history/comets-tale-63573615/

https://en.wikipedia.org/wiki/De_Havilland_Comet

http://www.who.int/ith/mode_of_travel/cab/en/

http://aerosavvy.com/aircraft-pressurization/

http://www.airspacemag.com/ist/?next=/flight-today/how-things-work-cabin-pressure-2870604/

http://edition.cnn.com/2011/TRAVEL/04/04/airplane.cabin.pressure/

http://news.bbc.co.uk/onthisday/hi/dates/stories/october/19/newsid_3112000/3112466.stm

http://www.sciencealert.com/watch-there-s-a-scientific-reason-for-why-aeroplane-windows-are-always-round

http://bgr.com/2016/01/15/why-airplane-windows-are-round/

http://mashable.com/2016/01/20/round-airplane-windows/

http://io9.gizmodo.com/why-is-there-a-hole-in-airplane-windows-1703660371

http://www.travelandleisure.com/articles/airplane-window-hole

http://time.com/3903109/airplane-window-holes/

http://www.skyscanner.net/news/secret-pilot-21-air-travel-truths-revealed

http://usatoday30.usatoday.com/travel/columnist/getline/2004-12-27-ask-the-captain_x.htm

http://www.independent.co.uk/travel/why-planes-dim-their-lights-when-landing-a6897516.html

Chapter 21

http://edition.cnn.com/2006/TECH/science/05/26/chicken.egg/

http://www.npr.org/sections/krulwich/2013/02/11/171706769/the-egg-makes-its-move-in-a-new-version-of-which-came-first-the-chicken-or-the-e

http://hubpages.com/education/ChickenEggFirst-Greensleeves

https://en.wikipedia.org/wiki/Chicken_or_the_egg

www.ingramcontent.com/pod-product-compliance
Lightning Source LLC
Chambersburg PA
CBHW071351280526
45787CB00001B/284